Malveaux,

May God "Days

Wit   + your

Family.

Eddie Hinton
8/20/99

LOCKER ROOM

TO

BOARDROOM

**SUPER BOWL PLAYER EDDIE HINTON'S
STRATEGIES FOR TACKLING LIFE'S CHOICES,
CHALLENGES, AND CHANGES**

The beauty of Eddie's story is the evolution in his life, the growth and strength he developed within himself. A very good story for young athletes . . .

> *Cleo Glenn Johnson*
> *Concerned Mother of Two*

This book shows how a person can be successful if they use the God-given talents they possess.

> *Jerry Logan*
> *Director of Judges*
> *National Cutting Horse Assoc.*

. . . motivating and inspiring. Eddie's story is one that will be enjoyed by all.

> *Dan Lawson, President*
> *Lawson Bus Manufacturing*
> *Company*

. . . the story of a winner!

> *Richard Hunton*
> *Chief Executive Officer*
> *Houston Trane*

LOCKER ROOM
TO
BOARDROOM

SUPER BOWL PLAYER EDDIE HINTON'S STRATEGIES FOR TACKLING LIFE'S CHOICES, CHALLENGES, AND CHANGES

He escaped from "Bootlegger Alley," donned the coveted uniform of professional football, and survived the chasm of transition from the world of sports to the world of business.

As Told To
LYNNE WASHBURN

CANDLE PUBLISHING COMPANY SUGAR LAND, TEXAS

LOCKER ROOM TO BOARDROOM

SUPER BOWL PLAYER EDDIE HINTON'S
STRATEGIES FOR TACKLING LIFE'S CHOICES,
CHALLENGES, AND CHANGES

Published by:
Candle Publishing Company
P.O. Box 5009-136
Sugar Land, Texas 77487-5009
(713) 242-6162

A
CANDLE
BOOK

Library of Congress Cataloging-in-Publication Data
Hinton, Eddie, 1947–
    Locker room to boardroom: Super Bowl player Eddie
Hinton's strategies for tackling life's choices, challenges, and
changes / as told to Lynne Washburn.
      p. cm.
    Summary: Traces the life and multiple careers of the black
football player who successfully made the transition from
professional sports to the business world.
    ISBN 0-942523-34-2.   ISBN 0-942523-33-4 (pbk.)
    1. Hinton, Eddie, 1947–   . 2. Football players—United
States—Biography. 3. Businessmen—United States—Biography.
[1. Hinton, Eddie, 1947–   . 2. Football players. 3.
Businessmen. 4. Afro-Americans—Biography.] I. Washburn,
Lynne, 1942–
II. Title.
GV939.H53A3 1988
796.332′092′4—dc19
[B]
[92]

DEDICATION

TO THE UNIVERSITY OF OKLAHOMA:

HAPPY 100TH BIRTHDAY!

1890 – 1990

Thank you for the honor of wearing
the crimson and cream uniform.
I am especially grateful for your gifts of
guidance, encouragement, wisdom, and love;
and I thank God for the privilege
of being a part of Sooner history.

Eddie Gerald Hinton, #33
Class of 1970

"Everything in the past is just a trace in our brain and we remember not what really occurred but how our brain conveniently wants to arrange it; and that tomorrow is a fantasy in our minds which never turns out how we fantasize it, whether good or bad; and that the only time that matters is today."

Kendrick Mercer

CONTENTS

PART II

PART III

ACKNOWLEDGMENTS

This book began as a writing seminar project and quickly became a challenge of completion.

I wish to thank Eddie Gerald Hinton for his patience, moral support, and love. He shared his soul with me in the telling of his story.

To my parents, Charles and Mary Washburn: Thank you for the honor of our family name and for bringing me up in the way I should go.

Thank you, Chuck, for our past. Your contribution to my life is beyond the realm of words.

Thank you, Jordan and Gina, for allowing me to be who I am.

I wish to thank my writing coaches, Elizabeth and Jerele Neeld, for their encouragement, integrity, and wisdom.

Special thanks to my faithful staff, Wanda White, Carol Estes and Evelyn Ellison, for their trust in me, themselves, and the worthiness of the project.

Lynne Washburn

FOREWORD

For those who have never seen Eddie Hinton play football, the records section of the O.U. media guide gives you a pretty good idea of what he was capable of doing when he stepped on the field. He holds the all-time record at Oklahoma for passes caught in a career and in a single season.

For those who were lucky enough to see him perform, I'm sure you remember those great hands, the sprinter's speed, and the versatility that allowed him to contribute as a running back, a wingback, a punt returner, and even a defensive back. His skills carried over into professional football where he carved out an outstanding career in the NFL.

Those are the things you have seen or read about. But for Eddie Hinton, the records on the field are barely adequate in comparison to Eddie Hinton off the field.

I first came into contact with Eddie after coming to Oklahoma as an assistant coach in 1966. He was just entering his sophomore year but was already something special, a quality that became obvious to those who watched him play and to others of us who came into contact with him on a day-to-day basis.

It may seem somewhat maudlin to talk about player-coach relationships, but I find that as time passes, it is far more rewarding to see how my players do after their final game here at Oklahoma than all the victories we have been fortunate enough to achieve here. The relationships that begin on the football field then carry over and solidify throughout the years are the most valuable I have.

Through the years Eddie Hinton has been a perfect example of that kind of positive relationship. He was the first great black athlete I was ever associated with and as time passed, we became good friends away from the game. The affection and respect we have for each other goes far beyond the boundaries of football.

His drive and self-confidence in every phase of his life are both extraordinary and exemplary. His path from a poor black kid growing up in Lawton, Oklahoma to the position of entrepreneur in present day society is a story that can't help but inspire those who read it.

I am delighted with his success and extremely proud of his accomplishments. I hope you enjoy his story. I think you will, and then can understand why Eddie Hinton holds such a special place in my heart.

Barry Switzer

Barry Switzer

PREFACE

The so-called "game" of football is a highly complex, multi-million dollar business with powers so great that it can fulfill a young man's dreams on a lucky bounce of the ball or it can devastate his future on an incompleted pass.

I was in the fifth grade when I was formally introduced to the game of football. Back then, it was merely recreation, but now I realize that it kept me off the streets of destruction. Through the game, I learned about setting goals, and competing *with* myself as well as *for* myself.

Using the game of football as a stepping stone, I accepted a four-year athletic scholarship to The University of Oklahoma. My interest in education increased as I played, because my self-confidence grew with each measurable victory. I began to improve my mind as I improved my body.

One day, football allowed me to go another step further in my life. In 1969, I was the number one draft choice of the Baltimore Colts. It seemed too good to be true that I would be financially rewarded for playing with teammates such as Johnny Unitas, John Mackey, and many other great athletes.

As each season came to a close, every game became more important than the one before. The tension and fear of defeat grew stronger, which caused me to push beyond the limits of physical, mental, and emotional exhaustion.

The night before Super Bowl V, I told myself that I was going to give 110% the next day. I recall looking up at the sky and whispering a familiar athlete's prayer: "O Lord, they say it's just a game!"

What I didn't know then was that life would always be like a Super Bowl game—that there would always be challenges, opponents, teammates, goals, losses, rewards, fumbles, victories, and the opportunity to learn and grow.

I want to thank all the people who helped me become who I am. Perhaps through my story, others can call forth their inherent magnificence, their long-forgotten dreams, and the unspeakable joy of playing in this greatest game of our lives, the infinite Super Bowl.

Eddie G. Hinton

PROLOGUE

The meeting room was on its final morning yawn as I entered. The crisply draped tables looked like white lily pads floating on a mossy pond. The smell of bacon and coffee from the sumptuous buffet crept through my nose and into my stomach. Big Girl's chubby, brown face suddenly appeared in my mind, and my throat constricted momentarily.

Get hold of yourself, Hinton. You've got an announcement to make, so don't let the smell of home cookin' and a few precious memories blow it.

"This sure looks good, doesn't it?" I said to the sleepy-eyed guy behind me, hoping the small talk would get my attention back to the impending meeting. He mumbled his agreement about the food selection as I turned to the waitress and ordered a plate of scrambled eggs, bacon, biscuits, and hash browns.

That's right . . . get your mind on the food and the business at hand.

The lily pad tables were sprouting suits and ties around their edges. I peeled out of formation in the buffet line and made my way to a red-cushioned seat near the front of the room. I exchanged warm greetings with the other three men already seated at the table. They were in various stages of consuming their breakfast and were discussing the day's business activities. I tuned my internal radar so that I could eat, converse with them, and survey the room. It looked like most of the eighty members were present this morning.

That's good . . . they'll all know at once.

There was a variety of sizes, shapes, and shades, but all participants had at least two things in common: We had distinguished ourselves by succeeding in our businesses and we were there to share our knowledge. The Whitehall Club was one version of America's new emerging business and professional marketplace—networking. The members met to exchange ideas and to refer business opportunities to each other.

Tailored, talced, and trimmed, each of us was a statement of early-morning discipline. I wondered if their daily routine was anything like mine. At 4:45 that morning I had donned jogging clothes, run two miles, showered, shaved, and ironed my shirt. After making the bed, scanning the paper, and guzzling a quart of orange juice, I headed for the freeway and jockeyed into position among a million people all trying to get somewhere by 7:00 am.

"What time you got, Henry?" I asked my table partner. Henry was a highly respected venture capitalist and, like me, was known to enjoy the finer things in life.

"It's twenty 'til eight," Henry reported amiably, glancing at his diamond-studded Piaget watch.

It's almost time, Hinton, now just calm down!

At last, Chester Brewster, the program director, clanked his water glass with a spoon to get everyone's attention. "Okay, guys, let's get started," he urged, as the noise quickly subsided and members took their seats.

"Good morning, gentlemen!" Chester smiled from the podium. "Welcome to The Whitehall Club and thank you for being here." Chester was an executive vice president of one of Houston's largest independent oil companies. "The first thing we want to do is welcome the newcomers, and the second thing we want to do is remind you of our weekly meetings which are held right here every Friday morning at 7:15."

He flipped his notes to the next page and quickly introduced the two new members and the categories they represented. After a round of welcoming applause, he checked his agenda and proceeded. "Now," he said with a note of finality for old business, "let's go around the room and see who's been networking this week. Jim, looks like you're first."

Jim stood up at his table and gave an account of his networking activities. As he talked, I studied the faces of the men who represented a variety of occupations. I wondered if the creases on their foreheads were a result of executive stress, or if they had acquired them under the infamous hot sun of Houston's many golf courses.

Almost every business and professional category was covered. There was Henry, the venture capitalist; a plastic surgeon; a Rolls Royce/Cadillac dealer; the president of a bank; a commercial real estate mogul and about 75 others; each representing a primary business or professional category. As owner of Fly-Clean, Inc., I was the only mobile aircraft cleaning service company on the member roster. Whenever they wanted their airplanes, cars, buildings, or oil rigs cleaned, they called me.

I was also the only black in the room except for the waiters and waitresses. This scenario was not unusual for me, nor did it bother me. I didn't think of myself as a color, but rather as Eddie Hinton, a person.

Besides being the only black participant in the meeting, I was also the only ex-professional football player-turned-entrepreneur. I rather enjoyed these two distinctions—almost everyone knew who I was.

As the conversation made its way towards me, I mentally practiced my announcement. When I had that down pat, I reviewed all I could remember from my National Speakers' Association training. I located Bill, Gene, Frank, and David in the audience so I could acknowledge them when it was my turn to speak. Outwardly, I made sure my composure and confidence were visible, but inwardly, it was all I could do to sit still.

Hurry up, you guys, before I forget how I'm gonna say this!

"Okay, Eddie," Chester finally said, "it's your turn. You sure are looking spiffy this morning!" he complimented as I stood up.

"Well, thank ya' Chester!" I grinned, as I automatically straightened my tie for the forty-eleventh time. Usually I wore a sports jacket and slacks to the meetings, but today I had on my best suit.

They should see me in my work clothes when I get through washing the greasy belly of an airplane!

"I got two jobs this week from the members," I began in my best speaking voice. "One from Gene Hodges to clean and wax his wife's Mercedes, and one from Bill Samuels to clean a hangar at Hobby Airport which resulted in a one-year contract. Thank you, guys," I said, as I pointed them out in the audience. "I appreciate the referrals. On the other side, I sent a friend of mine to Frank Galbraith for some liability insurance, and one of my customers needed an accountant, so I referred him to David Weatherspoon. That wraps up my report," I concluded.

Instead of sitting down, I took a deep breath and continued. "I also have an announcement to make this mornin'," I said enthusiastically. The expectant silence confirmed everyone's attention. "I'm happy to be able to share my good news with the members of this club, 'cause y'all have helped me so much in my business," I said sincerely. "After nine years of washin' airplanes in the hot summer sun and freezin' my buns off in the winter time, I'm proud to announce that I'm takin' Fly-Clean public!"

Chester, recovering from the surprise addition to his agenda, started an enthusiastic round of applause and my ears perked up at the familiar sound. "That's great news, Eddie!" he exclaimed. "When can we hear more about this? How long you been working on it?" he asked excitedly.

I wanted to say, *Oh, just all my life, that's all!* Instead, I said "Well, it's taken a little over six months to get all the paperwork done, but I couldn't say anything 'til it was official. You know how these things go sometimes," I concluded.

"I'll tell you what, Eddie," Chester said, glancing at his watch, "we're going to run short on time if we don't keep moving, but why don't you be our speaker at the meeting two weeks from today and tell us all about this new venture. I'm sure all of us would like to hear about that process."

"Sure, I'll be glad to," I replied instantly. "You know how much I love to talk!" I laughed. "It'll be my pleasure!"

When the meeting was over, the crowd thinned quickly as members scurried to their respective offices, secretaries, and *Wall Street Journals*. The few members who weren't in a hurry gathered around me and offered their hearty congratulations. It felt like I was being initiated into something, but I wasn't sure what.

Well, you did okay, Hinton. Now it's time for ***you*** *to get back to your buckets, 'cause you gotta prove yourself again. It's all gonna be up to you, home-boy!*

———◆———

Getting to The Whitehall Club was a long journey for Eddie Hinton. No one told him how to get there — he just knew he didn't want to follow in his mother's footsteps.

From bootlegger's son to athletic acclaim at The University of Oklahoma, he gathered his creed for living along the way. What he hadn't learned in the alleys of Lawton, Oklahoma, he learned as a wide receiver in the locker rooms of professional football.

After a Super Bowl ring and a winning football career, time ran out on the "good-life" clock. *Real life* became his stadium, and he was the only one to call the plays. There were no huddles, no teammates, no family left. Everything he had lived for, prayed for, disappeared with the applause. At 27, Eddie Hinton had to learn to live again.

He stood on the edge of the chasm between pro sports and the rest of his life. It was a long way down and too broad to jump. Like other athletes before him, he lost his footing and plunged into the darkness of the chasm. Some never come out, but Eddie Hinton did.

A small plaque from a friend provided Eddie's first foothold for the precarious climb back to the sunlight. Goethe's words still hang on his living room wall as a reminder of the turning point in his journey: "Just trust yourself, then you will know how to live."

When an idea for a unique business appeared in the sky, he had to put that trust to the test. The meager capital he had was the change in his pocket, but the desire to excel was back in his heart. He entered the world of business only to find greater competition there than in the big-business world of professional football.

Both in and out of the boardroom, he found new arenas in which to play; unknown challenges on unfamiliar turf; and ways to keep the game from ending. Eddie Hinton leaves winning and losing to the "Cosmic Scorekeeper" and plays life as if it were the Super Bowl.

Locker Room to Boardroom is one man's story of escape from the chasm; and everyone's story of making childhood dreams come true.

PART ONE

Everything in the past is just a trace in our brain and we remember not what really occurred but how our brain conveniently wants to arrange it. . . .

1

BOTTLE WASHIN' BABY

It didn't seem important to me at the time, but I was born with a protective skin pigment called "black." Of course, if I'd been born any other color, my folks would've been very surprised. My mom, Geraldine Hinton, was a roly-poly 17-year-old maid with an eighth grade education; and my dad, Eddie L. Hinton, was a 22-year-old Army cook. He was tall, slender, and hesitant about everything.

I wasn't much interested in what was going on in the world on that day of my birth in 1947, but if I'd been able to read the newspapers, I might have picked up some good news and bad news about the life that lay ahead of me.

The bad news was mostly about the effects of World War II. It was barely over and an estimated 35 million lives had been snuffed out, plus another 10 million people had perished in Nazi concentration camps. What a "Welcome to the world, Eddie!"

On the other hand, there was some good news that would eventually impact my journey through life.

The theatre was featuring Compton Mackenzie's "Whisky Galore," but I was too innocent to know that my choices in life would revolve around this abundant liquid commodity . . .

Jackie Robinson was the first black to sign a contract with a major baseball club, but I was too little to imagine that sports would play a role in my own search for identity . . .

The Dead Sea Scrolls were discovered in Wadi Qumran, but I had no inkling that I would enter and escape from a dark, dangerous chasm of self-destruction . . .

The first U.S. airplane flew at supersonic speeds, but it was much too early to predict that someday I would land in a business career related to aviation.

We lived in Lawton, Oklahoma, a small city in the southwestern quadrant of the state. Lawton was the home of Ft. Sill, the nation's top Army artillery training base. Daddy was stationed at Ft. Sill and his job was to cook for the soldiers. I guess it was his home away from home, since he didn't live with us.

I don't remember much about Daddy, because he stayed gone most of the time. So at the very beginning, there was just me, Mom, and Grandmother Odessa.

Grandma was a tough old babe—she dipped snuff, cussed a blue streak, and, mercy, could she hustle folks! She knew what she wanted and most of the time, she gave direct orders to get it! She was also loving and kind when it fit her needs.

Mama worked as a maid during the day for a prominent Lawton family. She cleaned, cooked, and cared for them while Grandma did the same for me. Daddy came to visit us a couple of times a year, but I don't recall talking to him much. He and Mama always had a lot of catching up to do when he came home for his short visits, so I instinctively minded my own business when he was around. Then one day, Mama went to something called a hospital and came back with my baby brother, Walter.

The Hintons were different than most people in the neighborhood, because we had two houses and a great big yard. The big house in front was named "Geraldine's Place" after my mom, even though we all lived there; and the little house in back was where Grandma and I worked.

Grandma's little house only had two rooms and half a kitchen. There was a deep cast-iron sink and some rough, splintery counter space. There wasn't a stove or refrigerator, though. Around the walls of the dusky rooms, there were stacks of yeast and sugar bags that looked like giant pillows. I would've loved to bounce on them and climb the mound all the way to the ceiling, but Grandma kept a close eye on her "mixin's." She wouldn't have hesitated a minute to wallop me soundly for playing mountaineer on her sugar and yeast pinnacles.

For the longest time, I thought Grandma was a cook like Daddy, although she never seemed to need a stove for her work. She mixed the two white, powdery ingredients together in what she called "croaker sacks." Then she dumped the mixture of sugar and yeast into huge brown earthen crocks and added water to a certain level. Within a few hours, it began to bubble and smell real sweet, almost like fresh bread dough. At some magic moment that only Grandma knew, the frothy brown liquid turned into what she called "chock." She'd smell it, taste it, and hold a jarful up to the light. When she said, "Mighty fine, mighty fine!" I knew it was time for me to go hunting.

My first job at the mature age of six or seven was to search the ditches, alleys, and trash cans of Lawton for bottles to put the chock in. When Walter got to be four, he was old enough to go with me. We left the house early in the morning with a tow sack between us. One of Daddy's old Army canteens kept us from dying of thirst in the heat of the Oklahoma sun. We filled the tow sack with whatever bottles we could find and dragged it back to

Grandma. She'd let us eat lunch and rest while she checked the bottle rims for chips or cracks.

During the afternoon shift, we washed the bottles with hot soapy water and some putrid-smelling green stuff. It wasn't much fun on a hot summer day, especially since we worked inside the little house and Grandma purposely kept the windows boarded up "to pertec' them bags from the daylight," she'd say.

After the bottles were given their afternoon bath, they had to be rinsed and rinsed and rinsed, then turned upside down in rusty metal racks to drain and dry in the sun behind the little house. I liked to make the bottles look new, but the rest of the job I didn't like. We got nicks and cuts and scratches all over our hands and forearms from the bottles; ant and chigger bites decorated our legs; the fear of deadly rattlesnakes was ever present; unfriendly dogs and grown-ups chased us out of their trash; and we received a much too early education about what one finds in gutters.

Walter and I each had our own galvanized dippers which we used for filling the squeaky-clean bottles. We had a capping tool for sealing, one-by-one, the endless racks of chock-filled containers. Grandma was always present, issuing orders on how to improve the quality of our work. She made us pile bed sheets on top of a case before it was moved to Geraldine's Place "to keep the sun off 'tween here and there," she'd say, "and if'n anyone ax you what you doin', you tell 'em you carryin' the laundry for your Grandmother."

With Walter on one side and me on the other, we lugged each case across the big yard, up the seven steps of the back porch and into the slightly less-hot kitchen. We neatly stacked the night's supply of chock next to the drink cooler. Then and only then, could we play until dark.

When night came on, the big house bulged with people Mama called customers. The customers gave Mama money, and she gave them Grandma's chock. There was something different about the people who came to Geraldine's Place. Some of them I knew as neighbors and some of them I felt I didn't want to know. All I knew was that everyone wanted some of Grandma's chock.

The "parties," as Mama called them, really got started about 10:00—just about the time Walter and I had to go to bed. The top bunk in our shared room was my favorite place in all the world, because it was the only place I could call my very own. When the parties got real noisy, I wrapped my pillow around the back of my head to cover my ears; and if I laid just right, it would stay in place so I could go to sleep.

I guess Walter and I were luckier than the other neighbor kids—at least, that's what they said. We always had new clothes and the latest toys. Grandma also gave us a fifty-cents-a-week allowance, which made me feel pretty grown up. I could buy my own candy or whatever I wanted! I didn't know what a piggy bank was, so I always had some pennies in my pocket. But there was something that bothered me: Even though we had the biggest yard, the newest toys, and the most spending money, the neighbor kids didn't come to play with us.

2

RETURN OF THE ARMY BRAT

Mama was home from work earlier than usual and was stocking the cooler with chock and soft drinks. She seemed to be in a pretty good mood, so I grabbed a grape Popsicle out of the freezer and perched myself on a bar stool near the cooler.

"Mama, how come Luther's parents won't let *him* play over here, but I see *them* in our livin' room almost every night drinkin' chock? Does that make any sense to you?" I asked, puzzled.

Mama slammed the cooler lid and whirled around, a startled look on her face.

"What you askin' for, Eddie Gerald?" she asked suspiciously. "Somebody done said somethin' ugly to you or Walter? Jus' tell me who, and I'll cut 'em off!" she snapped irritably.

"Don't get riled up, Mama," I soothed, wondering why this simple question was creating such a reaction. "I was just askin' 'cause it seems like nobody can ever come home from school with me," I explained hesitantly. "All they say is 'No, man, I can't come over—my mama won't let me.' I get tired of just playin' with Walter," I complained. A streak of purple, sticky Popsicle lava began its

6

flow down my wrist. I licked futilely while Mama gathered some clean ashtrays from the counter top and headed for the living room.

"Well, Eddie Gerald," she said over her vanishing shoulder, "you know how some folks are—they want their kids home after school to get their lessons. Fetch me a wet rag so's I can mop off these table tops," she ordered.

I slurped the last of the Popsicle from its stick and pivoted off the bar stool, trying not to touch anything on the way to the sink. Mama seemed upset, and the last thing I wanted to do was get her mad at me. The tap water was lukewarm as I splashed just enough water to get rid of the syrupy ring around my mouth.

Mama was speaking from the living room, but her voice was garbled over the sound of the running water. ". . . not gonna matter . . . neighbor kids no . . . movin' to Germany."

I squeezed the excess water from the rag so it wouldn't drip on the floor. When I went into the living room, Mama was sitting on the edge of the sofa, nervously fanning herself with a tattered magazine. The jukebox blinked in the corner, waiting to be fed.

"What'd you say, Mama?" I asked, approaching the sofa. "Sounded like you said we's movin' to Germany!" I laughed, trying to ease the tension that my question had somehow triggered.

She stood up and took the rag from my damp fingers, an unusual look on her face. "That's 'zactly what I said, Eddie Gerald. We's movin' to Germany!"

I started to laugh again, but the look on her face told me that would not be a smart thing to do. I stood there dumbfounded.

"Movin' . . .?" I whispered in disbelief, "you mean movin' outta this house?"

"Yes," she said flatly and my heart began to beat double-time.

"What for we movin', Mama?" I asked as if there might be a reason good enough to do such a thing. I desperately hoped she'd burst out laughing and say, "Boy, I gotcha this time! Fooled you, didn't I?"

Instead, she said matter-of-factly, "Your daddy's done been transferred to Germany and we's goin' with him."

My first silent reaction was, *Daddy? Daddy who? What right does Daddy have to move us away from here? He ain't around enough to matter—who does he think he is anyway?* My stomach knotted at the thought of leaving the very few friends I had. I knew Germany was far, far away and you had to cross the ocean to get to it. Surely there was some mistake.

"Germany, what, Mama? Germany, Mississippi?" I questioned, searching for *any* place that sounded closer to home.

"No, Eddie Gerald . . . you know . . . Germany, Europe!" she said with exasperation.

"You mean the one across the ocean? Are you sure it's *that* Germany?" I asked insistently.

"Yes, it's *that* Germany," she assured me emphatically.

There was nothing I could think of to say.

Mama turned away and began whisking the rag over the laminated table tops, not saying a word. As if in a hypnotic trance, I sat down where she'd been. The sofa was still warm from her body. The questions bounced around inside my head. *How can we move across the water? Why are we goin' with Dad? Why Germany? Why so far away?* I realized she was serious. This was not a joke.

My school books were stacked at one end of the couch, and the sight of them gave me an idea.

"What 'bout school, Mama?" I appealed innocently. "We're havin' our Easter play next month and I'm suppose to read a poem!" I informed her indignantly.

She continued to flap her rag at the table tops as I crossed my fingers and toes for luck.

"They have schools in Germany, Eddie Gerald—right there on the base where we'll be stayin'. 'Side's, we're not leavin' 'til the end of May, so you can still be in the play," she promised.

That one didn't work, so I frantically searched for other reasons we shouldn't go.

"What about Walter and Grandma? Are they goin', too? What about my friends?" I asked desperately.

"Well, 'course Walter's goin' with us!" she said impatiently. "Grandma ain't goin' though—she's gonna stay here to look after things; and you will make *new* friends in Germany," she assured me without a trace of doubt. Mama straightened the lamp shade and punched a lumpy cushion in the recliner.

"How we gonna get there?" I quizzed cautiously, thinking about my new bike and the toys in my closet.

Mama started to waddle toward the kitchen as the dust mites circled the lamps for another landing.

"I don't know yet if we'll be flyin' or takin' a big boat, but we'll get there, don't you worry. Your dad will let me know in due time. Soon's I know, we can start packin' up."

Her frame disappeared through the kitchen doorway and I heard the screen door bang like a judge's gavel as she went outside to call Walter for his bath.

No wonder Mama had been so quiet lately! No wonder she had been spending so much time on the phone talking to Daddy! I had gone in the house one day and heard her crying. "Jus' say you love me," she had sobbed into the receiver. "Can't you say it just once?" she had pleaded. Feeling guilty about listening in on her private conversation, I had quickly gotten a drink of water and bounded out the back door. There must be some connection between the move and the phone call, but what? Why?

I wanted to punch the cushion as Mama had done, but I wanted to pretend it was Daddy's face. I thought about running away from home, but that didn't make much sense under the circumstances. I wanted to scream at somebody who would listen. Instead, I leaned back wearily on the sofa and tried to pretend that I wasn't going to cry.

———◆———

The kids in my third grade class were gathered around the table at the back of the school room. There on the table was a present wrapped in plain white paper with a blue bow, and a poster hung on the wall that said "Good-Bye Eddie." A tray of peanut butter cookies and cups of orange Kool Aid waited patiently on the paper tablecloth.

The bell was going to ring at 3:20, the party would be over, and on Monday I'd be on my way to Kentucky. Everything was set. Daddy would meet us at the train station for a trip to New York's harbor. From there, we'd all ride on a huge ship to Germany.

Mrs. Walker smacked the table top with her blackboard pointer.

"All right, boys and girls," she yelled, ". . . settle down . . . Michael, take your place, please," she prompted.

Michael was my best buddy at recess. He probably would have come to my house after school if he had lived closer to me. Now there wouldn't be a chance.

He was always getting into trouble with the teacher, the girls, and the bigger boys—everyone except me. We sort of took care of each other, if we could.

The group quieted and crowded closer. Michael was squeezed out of his front-row position. Mrs. Walker placed a thick, white folder in my hands, and I wanted to grab her wrists and hold on. She was suddenly my favorite teacher, and I knew there were not going to be any Mrs. Walkers in Germany.

"Eddie Gerald, the class made these for you to read on the boat," Mrs. Walker began. "We hope you like them and will think of us often," she smiled warmly.

"Thank you," I murmured, as I took the gift and began to open it slowly. The booklet was titled "To Eddie Hinton from Dunbar 3rd Grade Class," and inside its scrawled cover were lots of Big Chief tablet pages. Each page was a printed letter from my classmates, decorated with pictures of boats; a waving hand outlined in brown Crayola; and a picture of the American flag.

When I looked up, everyone seemed to be waiting for me to say something. I wished the bell would go ahead and ring, but since it didn't, I said "Thank you" again.

Michael pushed his way to the inside of the circle, causing a chain reaction of shoving and giggling. He thrust another gift at me and in his best "Donald Duck" voice said, "Hurry up and open it, so we can have a cookie!"

The kids laughed and jostled each other for a bird's-eye view. Mrs. Walker handed me a pair of blunt-nosed scissors to cut the ribbon. Inside the box was a cream-colored fake leather scrapbook nestled in a bed of tissue paper. "MY TRIP" was printed in gold on the cover. Pencils, crayons, and a pair of scissors were tucked neatly beneath the book.

"We thought you'd like some place to keep all your souvenirs. You can even paste pictures of your new school and your new friends in it," Mrs. Walker said, somewhat sadly.

"That's nice," I lied politely, not wanting any new friends *or* souvenirs.

"Can we have our cookies now, Mrs. Walker?" Michael asked as he tugged at her skirt.

"Let Eddie get his first," she instructed, "then y'all can each have *one!* I don't want your mamas mad at me for spoilin' your dinners! Get your cookie, Eddie, then I'll pass out the Kool Aid."

————◆————

Walter stirred in the ocean of bed space we were sharing. We'd been in Lexington, Kentucky for two nights already, waiting for Daddy's orders. When I rolled over to see if Walter was awake, the vaccination shots we had unwillingly received the day before reminded me why I was in such a strange bed. We were leaving for Germany at noon.

Mama and Daddy were in the adjoining room. I could hear their muffled voices through the wall, and it sounded like Mama was crying. I could barely hear what Daddy was saying. ". . . please . . . well, . . . what you want . . . the boys . . . change your mind. . . ."

I pulled the cover over my head and buried my face in the hotel pillow. Maybe if I played dead, they'd leave me here and I could find my way back to Oklahoma. A door slammed and I heard footsteps clomping past our door and down the hall.

When I woke up again, Mama was in our room folding Walter's clothes and putting them in the suitcase. Walter was brushing his teeth at the funny looking bathroom sink. I stretched, sat up, and tried to rub the sleep from my face.

"Mornin' Mama. Is it time to go now?" I asked groggily.

"Yes, 'tis," she answered curtly. "Get up and get yourself dressed, Eddie Gerald. We need to be leavin' in about 30 minutes," she instructed. Her eyes looked kind of swollen and red, and I wondered what time it was.

"Can I wear my new boots to New York so I don't have to smash 'em in my suitcase?" I asked, still wallowing in the bed sheets.

She turned her face away and sighed heavily. "We ain't goin' to New York and we ain't goin' to Germany, neither—we's goin' back to Lawton," she announced unhappily. "Get out of that bed and get ready so's you can help me carry these suitcases!"

"Goin' back to Lawton?" I asked in disbelief. "Did you say we's goin' back to Lawton?" I bolted out of bed and almost landed on Mama. She was wrestling with the suitcase on the floor, trying to get it closed.

"That's what I said. We's goin' back to Lawton," she repeated monotonously.

"But . . . but what happened to Germany? What about movin'? Where's Daddy?" I demanded excitedly.

"Don't ask questions, boy!" she snapped. "Just do what I tol' you and get ready. We ain't goin' and that's all you need to know. Now hurry up, you two! We've got an Oklahoma train to catch!"

I knew better than to ask any more questions. I grabbed my boots from under the chair and headed for the bathroom. "Hurry up, Walter!" I ordered, jostling him out the door. "If you make us miss that train, you're gonna get it!"

The trouble between Daddy and Mama remained a mystery to me. Although I never knew what happened, I was glad to be running *towards* home rather than away from it.

3

BRIMSTONE AND BUCKSKIN

After returning from the trip to Germany that never happened, we settled back into a familiar pace at home. The summer stretched gloriously ahead of me and I began to look for fun ways to fill it up. The only shadow hanging over me was whether or not to return the going-away presents when school started in the fall.

When I wasn't working for Grandma, I was busy scrounging up enough kids to play marbles or, if it wasn't too hot, we would meet at the school yard for basketball, baseball, or football. Usually I got to be the captain of the team because I was the one with the best ball, bat, or mitt.

Most of my toys came from Daddy, or at least that's what I was told. For birthdays or special holidays, Mama would hand me a present and say, "Here, your dad wants you to have this." The way she said it left doubt in my mind as to whether it was really from Daddy or if she was just saying that to make me feel good. Sometimes she would give me money and say the same thing. I always accepted the gifts she offered, but there was a hollow feeling inside of me.

If the big earthen crocks were empty, making our bottle hunts unnecessary, Walter and I were allowed to go to the army base on Saturdays. There was always something going on inside those endless chain link fences. Ft. Sill had a commissary where military personnel and their families could shop, and almost every weekend there was some kind of parade. We could also swim during the summer and shoot pool in the winter. As far as I was concerned, the only advantage to having a father at all was having one in uniform.

One of the neighbor kids sold newspapers at the commissary, and I was impressed by his ability to make some real money. After carefully choosing my words, I asked Mama if I could work with him on weekends.

"Nope," she said stubbornly in the way that only Mama could, "I don't want my boys out there hustlin' money and people talkin' 'bout 'em."

"Well, can I shine shoes on the base then?" I pleaded insistently.

"Nope, don't want that either," she replied emphatically.

"Can I go caddy at the golf course? Robert's mom lets him go, and he makes lots of money," I added, thinking that my ten-year-old logic could persuade her.

"Nope, don't want people thinkin' I ain't takin' care of my children. I'll find somethin' 'round here for you to do and pay you for it," she offered in her stubborn take-it-or-leave-it way.

From then on, I was in charge of emptying the trash and cleaning up the house after her parties. It seemed like I'd been doing this most of my life anyway, but she assured me her wages were more than I could have made "hustlin'."

———◆———

Saturday afternoons were my favorite. After cleaning up Friday night's party mess, I was free for the rest of the day. When I was bored with Ft. Sill, I went to the movies.

The picture show closest to our house had Saturday matinees all day long. They showed cartoons in the morning for the little kids, and westerns in the afternoon. The double-double features only cost 50 cents, so I could watch hours and hours of Roy Rogers, Hopalong Cassidy, and the Lone Ranger.

Sometimes I'd find a friend who had enough money to go with me, but usually I went alone. Boy, did I have a good time! There was something thrilling about entering the cool darkness of the theater, the smell of freshly popped popcorn, and the thunderous sound of galloping horses.

One Saturday morning, I got through with my chores early and decided to explore some more of Lawton before heading to the movies. The alleys and back streets were familiar hunting territory, but in my search for bottles, I had never skirted the edge of town. Since I was alone and free from the responsibility of watching out for Walter, I chose a path that not only looked inviting but challenging! It disappeared into a grove of trees and its unknown destination excited me.

The trees were dressed in their full summer foliage and my footsteps were muffled by the grassy carpet as I made my way along the path. Unidentifiable scurryings in the underbrush reminded me that I was pretty far from home and made me wish Walter were there to keep me company. Whistling as I walked, my imagination took over and carried me out of Lawton and into the past I had seen on the movie screen. I was on a scouting mission for my wagon train, and all its passengers were depending on me to find a way through the dangerous forest. I stalked unseen Indians, forded rivers that had long since dried up, and climbed snowy mountain peaks that had never existed.

Suddenly, I heard a noise that didn't seem to be coming from the world of make-believe. I stopped, listened, and tried not to breathe. There it was again. It sounded like . . . no it couldn't be . . . yeah, it was! The familiar sound of horses prompted me to run. Ducking under low hanging branches and hurdling the small trunks of fallen trees, I rushed along the path as the sounds continued, ever closer. The path ended abruptly, and as I stopped to catch my breath, I saw a row of weather-beaten sheds. There was a commotion on the other side that drew me cautiously closer. I flattened myself against the rough planks of the crude structure and eased my way to the end of it so I could see what was going on. What I saw when I peeked around the corner of the shed made me think I'd died and gone to Heaven! Horses! Real live horses! Just like the ones I'd seen in the picture show! Well, *almost like the ones I'd seen in the movies*. These weren't slick and shiny and wild, but they were horses. It didn't matter to me that they were dusty and ridden by flies, or that they were obviously enjoying their standing afternoon siestas. I spotted some tattered saddles perched on the broken-down fence, and my heart raced in excitement. I made my way to what looked like the front of the place and saw a faded sign that said, "OK CORRAL—HORSE RIDES—$1.00/ HOUR."

Well, the sign could have been in neon lights as far as I was concerned! This was the most wonderful thing I had ever seen in Lawton! How had I missed this place?

I reached in my pocket and pulled out several lint balls and seventy-three cents! "Darn! Not enough," I moaned as I mentally kicked myself for having bought a soda the day before. A scheme emerged that was not satisfactory, but under the circumstances, it was the best I could do. "I'll get my allowance next Friday, but that's still not enough if I go to the movies today. Oh well, I can always watch TV and maybe I can work extra for Mama this week." My disappointment was replaced by the promise I made to myself: "I'll come back just as soon as I save enough money to ride."

I reluctantly returned to the path I'd followed and on the way back, I memorized every twist and turn of it so I could find my way to the "Corral" again.

Candy, popcorn, and the Saturday matinees moved way down on my list of priorities. All the money I earned that summer went to my personal OK Corral fund, except for a small portion set aside each week to eventually buy a cowboy hat. Since I'd never seen a Hollywood western star without one, I figured it was an absolute must if I wanted to learn to ride as good as they did.

Before summer was over, I rode every horse that lived at the OK Corral. I discovered that each one had a different personality, just like us people. I learned their names and memorized all their little quirks. Most of the time, the sleepy old nags ignored my heels in their flanks, but as the weather began to cool, they delighted me with their friskiness.

My favorite dream when I was alone in my bunk bed was about owning my own horse one day—I wanted a wild, black stallion that only I could ride! My prayers took on new meaning. I was sure that if I prayed hard enough, God would give me a horse for Christmas. It seemed quite natural to imagine Mama taking me outside on Christmas morning and saying, "Here's your Christmas present from your dad. He wants you to have it."

———◆———

When the weather was bad on the weekend and I couldn't ride, I'd pile up in front of our black and white television and watch a baseball or football game.

I'll never forget one of those Saturdays. During the many halftime commercials, there was a tear-jerker ad about the shortage of teachers in college; and, therefore, young minds going to waste. It made me stop and think for the first time about my future. I began to wonder what was going to happen to me after I finished high school; and what was college, anyway? How could a person like me get there?

When I started asking around, I found out that college was the next thing after high school. That is—if you had the money! Well, that left me out, or so I figured. Then someone whose name I don't even remember told me that since I didn't have any money, but I had shown some athletic ability, I should pick one of the sports and get serious about it. They said if I developed myself into an athlete, I might get chosen to go to one of those colleges on a scholarship, whatever that was; and from there, maybe . . . just maybe . . . I could become a professional athlete and get paid for playing my favorite sport. That sounded too farfetched to be true, so I continued to dream away the long summer days.

————◆————

Mama made us go to church every Sunday, even though she wouldn't go with us. It seemed rather strange to me that she refused. Whenever anyone from the church needed anything—food, money, or clothing—she always had something to give. When I asked her why she wouldn't go with us, she replied with one of her not-to-be-questioned answers. "People don't always have to be in church to understand God, and there's things that I have to take care of 'round here. That's why y'all are goin' and you make sure these two quarters go in the collection plate!" she threatened. It still didn't make sense, but Walter and I went at her command.

The Reverend Jones, according to some members of the congregation, was full of what they called "hell-fire and brimstone." I didn't understand what that was, but I knew he could make us laugh, cry, clap, and holler "Amen!" on cue. He could also get people to join the church, confess their sins, and give more money. I figured it would be nice if I was able to use his successful brand of persuasion on Mama whenever I wanted something. I watched him intently on Sunday mornings to see if I could pick up some clues on how to get her to do what I wanted.

The Reverend always wore a shiny black suit, a threadbare but crisp white shirt, and a bright red slash of tie that looked like a giant wound in the center of his chest. He would shout at us one minute, then lower his voice to a bare whisper. He would point towards the ceiling whenever he said "Heaven," then slam both fists down on the pulpit when he said "hell-fire!" He swayed back and forth on his heels, holding on to the pulpit as if it were his holy wooden dancing partner. When the sweat started to trickle at his temples, he pulled a spotless white handkerchief from his pocket and held it to his wrinkled brow as if it too were permanently injured.

Whenever I was alone, I practiced talking like the Reverend in hopes that God would give me some of whatever it was He gave Brother Jones. But when I tried his style of prayer, "thee" and "thou" and "hast" and "wilt" just didn't fit my Oklahoma vocabulary. His "Almighty God, Our Heavenly Father" was much too long a title for me to use everytime I wanted to talk to God, so I nicknamed Him "Big Fella." During my nightly bedtime prayers, I always asked Big Fella to guide me so I could be the person He wanted me to be. I also threw in regular, respectful requests for a wild black stallion.

———◆———

Sometimes, going to church wasn't much fun at all. Like the time I had to tell Grandmother Odessa good-bye.

My friends and I had a good game of football going when my cousin Sandra came barging out of the big house to interrupt the action. There were five of us—me, Walter, Michael, Freddie, and Larry.

"Eddie Gerald, you and Walter come here for a minute," she yelled in a weird-sounding voice. Sandra was two years older than me and was always trying to boss me around. Her eyes were red and Walter looked at me as if to say, "What now?"

We took our own sweet time, then trotted to the imaginary sideline where Sandra was impatiently waiting. When we reached her side, she started blubbering, just like a baby. I couldn't imagine what was wrong.

"Grandmother Odessa just died," Sandra blurted through her soggy handkerchief. She was too busy crying to see Walter and me exchange a puzzled look. I wasn't sure what she was talking about.

"Died?" I asked, unfamiliar with this term except for when the car stalled, and Mama cussed a blue streak. I wondered if Mama was cussing now?

Walter screwed up his face like Sandra's and began to beller. "Died?" I repeated louder. "You mean she went to live with God?" I asked, knowing full well what *that* meant. It meant she wouldn't be back and she'd be real happy forever and ever.

Sandra blew her nose and peered at me around the hanky's edges. She seemed to be surprised and annoyed that I wasn't crying like her and Walter. I knew I was going to miss Grandma, but I sure didn't feel like crying. I wanted to get back to the game—maybe Grandma could watch me play from her new home way up in the sky!

Sandra wiped Walter's runny nose and tried to comfort him by putting her arm around his skinny shoulders. "Ain't you gonna say anything?" she asked, looking at me accusingly.

"Well, yeah, I guess so," I responded uncertainly. "What am I supposed to do now?" I asked innocently. I didn't know whether to go home or finish the game or what.

"Eddie Gerald, you ain't got no heart!" she yelled hysterically. "All you care about is football! Your Mama's 'bout to pass out from cryin', and you don't know what to do? You make me sick!" she spat, as she turned and stomped towards the big house. Walter gave me a last look of uncertainty and trotted after her, blubbering all the way.

———◆———

The next day, the house was filled with people. They didn't come to Geraldine's Place as customers—they came to try and wake Grandma up. At least that's what they called it. I stayed outside as much as possible, but there wasn't anybody to play with. Even Walter stayed inside close to Mama and the table loaded with food. I guess they figured if Grandma woke up, she'd be hungry.

I knew she wasn't going to wake up, but I had a plan whereby she might be able to hear me one more time. The funeral was scheduled for the following day, and when I walked down the aisle of the church to her rose-colored casket, there would be no way she *couldn't* hear me.

The back porch became my cobbler's workshop. Mama had bought me some taps for the heels of my new shoes to keep me from wearing them out too quickly. Equipped with the hammer and a handful of tiny nails, I spent several hours tacking them onto my shoes in just the right spot. I tested them on the sidewalk and was thrilled when I heard the rhythmical clickety-clack. Yup! She'd hear me, all right!

The next morning, I took my time getting dressed in my Sunday suit and padded around the house in my socks until it was time to go.

Mama's friends and cousins and relatives I'd never seen before were huddled around her in the yard when I click-clacked across the porch and down the front sidewalk to get in the car.

Mama's mouth dropped open and she started towards me. I knew I was in trouble, but I didn't know how bad. "Eddie Gerald, get those taps off them shoes right now!" she demanded hoarsely. "You ain't 'bout to wear them to your Grandmother's funeral," she snapped, as she shoved me toward the house. "Hurry up, too!" she ordered. "We's leavin' in two minutes with or without you!"

I prayed silently that it wouldn't take me as long to get them off my shoes as it had to get them on. I didn't want to miss saying good-bye to Grandma.

————◆————

I sang in the church choir almost every Sunday just so I wouldn't have to sit with Walter while most of my friends sat with their moms and dads. I used to look out at the audience from the choir loft, pick a set of parents, and pretend they were mine. When my eyes met those of my make-believe family, I'd smile real big and they'd smile back—unaware of the pleasant game I was playing. I made it up that they were smiling because they were so proud of me.

Sometimes the songs we sang were upbeat and downright raucous; and sometimes they were mournful pleas for God's mercy that made it hard for me to swallow.

I slowly realized a painful truth by being in the choir: I knew I'd never make a great singer, 'cause I couldn't remember the words! However, even away from church, music beckoned me, and I gladly heeded its call.

Clifford, my oldest cousin, was an excellent saxophone player. I walked or rode my bike to his house as often as I could, just to listen to him practice. He was constantly telling stories of his travels to play in bands throughout the state, and most of his tales included women.

Playing the sax didn't look too difficult, so one day I asked him to let me try it. He was very patient with me, and before long, I learned to toot a tune or two. Belinda, the girl who lived next door to him, was also musically inclined and played the clarinet. She practiced with me, too, whenever Clifford could spare his sax. Our favorite duet was "Home On The Range," and when we finally had it memorized, we performed for her mom and dad. What I thought was my first step to stardom was shattered by her parents' tactful suggestion that I enroll in beginner band in the fall.

Since fifth grade, I had been part of the basketball, track, baseball, and football teams that practiced after school everyday as part of physical education. I loved to run the 100-yard dash, but the low hurdles were my favorite challenge. I was sure I could become a track star and get one of those scholarships I'd been told about.

If I followed Belinda's parents' advice and enrolled in band, I could be on the track and baseball teams. Playing football, however, was out of the question because if I was in the band, I'd have to march at halftime. Eliminating football from my sports activities was okay with me. I had played enough sandlot, recess, and phys-ed football to know that running over people was not my favorite thing, and getting hit by others was even less appealing.

4

FUTURE CHOICES

Practice for our school's track meet was over, and the muscles in my legs were cramped from running and jumping the hurdles.

The rest of the team had already gone to the locker room, but I was taking my time cooling down. My legs rebelled at the thought of walking home after so many hours of practice. When the pain finally subsided, I headed for the showers.

As I passed the bleachers, I saw Mr. Vickers coming out of the storage shed. Mr. Vickers was the head coach at Douglass, Lawton's all-black school. I'd seen him around our elementary school baseball games, and some of my friends' older brothers played for his team.

He saw me, too, and hollered.

"Hey, Eddie! Wait up! I wanna' talk to you."

I stopped and waited as he smiled his way towards me, juggling an armful of baseball equipment.

"Hello, Mr. Vickers! What are you doin' over in this neck of the woods?" I greeted politely.

"I just came over to borrow these extra bases from y'all's equipment room," he puffed as he dumped the bases in a pile at his feet. He took off his baseball cap with one hand and wiped his forehead with the other. "I'm tryin' to get my equipment lined up for fall before school's out," he explained. "Cain't get nothin' done through the summer, 'cause everybody 'cept me will be on vacation," he grinned.

"Yes, sir, it's gettin' about that time," I agreed, hoping he'd come to the point quickly so I could get on home.

"Say, Eddie, do you know yet which school you're goin' to next year?" he asked with concern. "You'll be graduatin' from sixth grade in a few weeks, and September will be here before you know it!" he said, as if I needed to be reminded. I'd been struggling for weeks with the all-important question, trying to make a decision that I wouldn't later regret.

"Well, no sir, I'm still thinkin' about it. Sometimes it seems like it'd be better to go to your school, 'cause that's where most of my friends are goin'; and then sometimes I think it'd be better for me to go to Central Junior, 'cause it's mixed. 'Sides, my cousins go to Central and they say they have a good band. Got good sports programs, too—baseball, track, basketball, football. . . ."

"Yeah, they do," he interrupted agreeably. "'Course, Douglass has all that too, and even though we have lots of good athletes, we can always find room for another one," he kidded, "and, like you said, most of 'em are your friends." He paused momentarily as if to let that sink in. When I didn't answer, he continued excitedly. "Say!" he exclaimed, "did you hear the good news? We're gonna have brand new baseball gloves for everyone on the team next year! I been waitin' a long time for those," he reflected proudly.

"Gee, that's great, Mr. Vickers," I congratulated. I had to keep moving so my legs wouldn't tighten up and Mr. Vickers began to pace with me.

"Yeah, the guys are really lookin' forward to the new mitts," he assured me. "It's important to break 'em in right, you know? You got to work it so it fits your hand just perfect," he demonstrated in thin air, "and then rub it with saddle soap to keep it soft. Then you put your name inside so everybody knows not to mess with it," he concluded with authority.

"Yeah, that's a good idea, Mr. Vickers," I replied. "I'll do that with the one I've got, but I doubt if it will keep my brother Walter from playin' with it," I chuckled. We stopped the pacing, but I continued to shift from one foot to the other, more from impatience than from pain. I was flattered by his offer to have me on his team, but his subtle pressure only added discomfort to such an important decision.

"Well, listen, Eddie," he said as he draped a protective arm around my sweaty shoulder, "I got to run now, but you call me if I can help you in any way. Choosing the school you want to go to is a major decision," he said gravely.

He pulled a pencil stub and a crumpled piece of paper from his shirt pocket and wrote some numbers on it.

"Here's my phone number at home in case you want to call me after school's out. By the way," he continued as if it were an afterthought, "do you need a ride home?" he asked as he handed me the paper. "I'm goin' that direction."

"No, sir, thanks anyway. I've gotta shower and pick up my books from my locker. Besides," I grinned, "the walk will be good for me."

"Okay, then. Well, I'll be stayin' in town all summer, Eddie. Give me a call now, if I can be of any help," he waved, as he hurried to gather the pile of borrowed bases.

———◆———

In a way, I felt like I had let Mr. Vickers down, but come September, I entered the integrated junior high school with my saxophone in hand and my sports reputation tagging along behind. During the summer, my athletic abilities improved a lot faster than my musical skills. I was extremely proud of being the first to be chosen for sandlot teams, but slightly disappointed that no one asked me to play any sax solos.

The adjustment from an all-black school to an integrated junior high wasn't as bad as I had expected. The main difference, as far as I could tell after my first two weeks, was that Central was just bigger; there were about twice as many kids; and most of them were white. I got along well with everybody and wondered why I'd ever been worried about fitting in.

School days started early for me. During the summer, Mama let me earn some extra spending money at a place next to ours called John's Barbecue. Mr. Weathers, the owner, paid me for sweeping and mopping the floors, cleaning the ashtrays and taking out the trash. At five o'clock every morning, I was on my way next door to work; and by 8:20, I had to be in my first class.

For the next three years, Central was my home-away-from-home. Everyday seemed to be a repeat of the one before it. Up at five, over to John's, off to school, practice sports, do homework, clean the house, and fall in bed.

There wasn't much time to be with my friends, except during school hours. It didn't matter anyway—I rarely invited anyone to our house, or should I say Geraldine's Place, because I never knew who might be hanging around our living room.

———◆———

I awoke in the darkness with all five senses on sudden alert. The usual party voices from the living room were strangely absent, although the dream-muffled scream that awakened me had seemed to come from that direction.

The jukebox was blaring "Oh, Lonesome Me" and I could hear Walter's adolescent snores from the bunk below.

There! There it was again! I decided to go see what, if anything, was going on. I climbed down from my top bunk and eased the bedroom door open. It looked like the place was deserted and then I saw them on either side of Mama near the kitchen. Her face was contorted in pain and the two men flanking her looked very unhappy. One of them tried to lift her off the floor by her glossy black hair while the other one twisted her arm behind her back. I was frozen in disbelief and paralyzed by the sudden gush of ice water that seemed to surge through my veins. I don't know how long I watched the movie-screen horror before my instincts took over and I heard my voice in a croaking whisper.

"Walter! WALTER!! WAKE UP. Get over here! Hurry! Wake up! They're beatin' up on Mama! Hurry up . . . HURRY!" He leaped out of bed and scrambled to the door, dragging the tangled bed sheets with him. He almost knocked me down in his attempt to see what was going on.

He gasped at the sight of violence as he whirled around and flung his frightened arms about my waist. "Oh, Eddie!" he sobbed into my chest. "What we gonna do if they kill her? What we gonna do?"

"I don't know, Walter, I DON'T KNOW! Just shut up a minute so's I can think. One thing's for sure," I whisper-yelled, "we're gonna have to take care of ourselves if we don't stop 'em!" He let go of me and turned back to the door frame for support. He peeked through the crack bravely and again turned to me. "Oh, stop 'em! STOP 'em!" Walter begged, pulling me toward the door as if I could do something. I peered frantically into the darkness of the bedroom, trying to remember where I'd put my baseball bat.

"Eddie!" Walter hissed over his shoulder. "Looks like they's leavin'!" he squeaked with a note of childish hope. I ran back to the door just in time to see the men grab their cigarettes and beer bottles from the table as they sauntered toward the front door.

"We'll be back, Geraldine," the short one snarled nastily as he slammed the screen door behind them. We stood there motionless as the jukebox continued its mournful lament.

Mama clutched the counter and stiffly groped for a towel. She wiped her face and reached for the empty money box lying on the floor. She jerked the jukebox cord from its socket and stumbled into her room. Walter slumped against me, crying silently in relief. His earlier question slammed around inside my head. What *would* we do if something happened to Mama, as it almost did tonight. Thank God, she was all right this time, but what if, next time. . . .

We didn't have any relatives who could afford to take care of us; nor did we have any friends who wanted two more mouths to feed. The thought of turning to my father if she died never even occurred to me.

The next morning, we acted like we hadn't seen anything, although I desperately wanted to tell her we had witnessed the terrifying event. Mama didn't say a word about her ordeal—she was just unusually quiet and moved rather stiffly through her early morning routine. I didn't ask any questions, either—I was afraid she would ask me why I didn't help her.

———◆———

For Christmas that year, Mama gave me a shiny, deadly .22 caliber rifle. It was supposed to be for hunting, but the kind of hunting I did only required a good eye and a strong tow sack. However, I loaded it that day, and from then on, it slept with me in the top bunk.

I walked in the house one evening after baseball practice, and there in the middle of the living room floor was a mound of rolling, tumbling flesh. It was Mama and a woman customer I knew as Gloria. I'd been around this kind of stuff long enough to know that when people used fighting as a way to settle their differences, someone usually got hurt.

Walking straight to my bedroom, I pulled the rifle out from under the covers, cocked it, and strode silently into the living room. They were still on the floor, screaming and cussing and pulling each other's hair.

"Someone is gonna get killed while y'all are fightin', and I just want you to stop it! If you don't stop, I'm gonna kill someone and it ain't gonna be my mother!" I bellowed loudly over their disgusting noises.

They immediately stopped tussling at the sight of me and froze in position before the cocked rifle. I said a silent prayer as they sat there staring at me. I'd had enough of Geraldine's Place. I hated her business, her customers, and her product.

"We didn't mean no harm, Eddie Gerald," Mama said breathlessly, breaking the silence. "We jus' havin' a slight disagreement—tain't nothin' serious enough for no rifle," she said convincingly. "If you'll just point that thing the other way, we'll get up from here so's Gloria can go home."

I lowered the rifle slowly and said another silent prayer.

Mama rolled away from Gloria and pushed herself up off the floor. "You can put that thing away, now," she said, motioning me to my bedroom. "We'll talk 'bout this some other time, right Gloria?" Mama prompted through clenched teeth.

"Sho' nuff, Geraldine," Gloria replied as if they were best friends. "I meant no harm t'ya," she said as she smoothed her scrambled hair. The fixed smile never left her chalky face as she backed towards the door.

———◆———

That night as I lay in my bed, the cold, hard steel of the rifle pressed into my side. As I waited for sleep, I heard Walter say from the bottom bunk, "Eddie, you asleep? You sure was brave today, gettin' them apart," he said with admiration.

My jaw tightened as I controlled the urge to answer him. I didn't feel the least bit brave. All I knew was, I didn't want to grow up without a mother, and I didn't ever want to have to be the one to take care of us.

5

DRIVIN' THROUGH DALLAS

"Whatcha pullin' over for, Mama? We got a flat tire or sumthin?" I asked hopefully. I had already spotted a Stop 'N Go near the freeway where I could buy the latest *Sports Illustrated* to read on the rest of the trip. Mama, Walter, and I were on our way to Meridian, Mississippi to see my other grandmother, "Mama Bay."

"Naw, son, I jus' gots to have me a little nap," Mama yawned. "I gets soooooo sleepy drivin'. I jus' gonna pull off here for a jiffy and close my eyes," she said, as she turned her massive head to check the traffic behind and beside our new Pontiac.

"Can me and Walter run over to that there Stop 'N Go and use the bathroom and get us a Pepsi while you's asleep?" I asked politely. I was afraid if I said "magazine," she'd say no for sure.

"No, you cain't," she replied flatly, "'cause you's gonna drive and Walter's gonna ride shotgun while I lay up in the backseat."

"Oh, Mama, you're so funny," I laughed hysterically. When I could finally catch my breath after laughing so hard, I repeated my question. "Can we, huh? We won't be

33

gone too long, and we'll be real quiet when we come back to the car, in case you're still asleep," I promised.

"Didn't you hear what I said, boy? You're gonna drive and Walter's gonna help you," she stated again impatiently.

"MEEE?! DRIVE? IN THIS TRAFFIC? You can't be serious!" I exploded in total disbelief. "I'm only 14 years old! I ain't got no real license—it's just a permit to drive to school! I ain't never drove on no freeway before! I'd sure-to-God get us . . ."

"You better shut yo' mouth, boy! You gettin' me all riled up and I done tol' you I's sleepy! All you got to do is follow them signs up there what say Highway 80! Mama Bay is awaitin' for us in Meridian, and I want to get there by dark! We got to keep movin'!"

The car glided to a stop and she began to shift her hulk in the direction of the backseat. Walter started to whine and poked my arm through the crack between the seat and the car door.

"But, Mama," I pleaded in one last attempt at sanity, "what if I get stopped? What if I run into somebody and get us all killed??!"

"Boy, you better getchur' self in that driver's seat and herd this thing down that highway. If you learn to drive through Dallas, you can drive through anywhere. 'Sides, if you rile me so much I cain't go to sleep, you better hope some Mack truck saves you the misery of runnin' into my hand! Walter, shut up that blubberin' and get up front! You got to help your brother watch them signs!"

She swung the car door open and squirmed out of the car. Walter was breathing down the back of my neck, but at least he wasn't blubbering anymore.

Remembering well what her massive hand could do to a cheekbone, I chose the dangers of the freeway and started out of the car. My legs felt like warm rubber.

Walter scrambled over the seat to ride shotgun and I started to pray. I nervously made my way around the back of the car, jerked open the door, and crumpled into the driver's seat as an 18-wheeler barrelled past us.

"Fix your rearview mirror now and get to movin'," Mama ordered from the backseat. I heard the familiar "pshhh" as she uncapped one of her own home brew bottles. The familiar malty smell of the frothy liquid floated somewhere between my nose and the steering wheel. My stomach queased. I knew she'd have it downed, belched, and would be snoring before I could get across the two lanes of traffic to the spaghetti loop and the signs we had to follow.

I *hoped* I would be going to Meridian today and *not* to heaven or hell! I often thought about where I would go when I died. Did I really have any say so about it? Can blacks even get in?

"I'll find out *someday,* but it ain't gonna be today!" I said, talking under my breath as I gunned the reluctant Pontiac into the Dallas torrent of traffic. I felt the sweat trickling at my ears, armpits, and groin. Walter was gripping the dashboard with both hands, his eyes wide open in search of signs.

———◆———

My relationship with Mama had changed a lot since her wrestling match with Gloria. She treated me more like a grown-up, except for the ridiculous "vacations" she arranged for me and Walter.

One summer, she took us to stay with a family that did not have a refrigerator or a stove and couldn't even imagine what a washing machine was. They lived by a dump yard—a garbage pit—pigs and all. I couldn't understand it. Walter and I would take turns asking each other, "Why in the world would she leave us here?"

Another summer, she took us to Chickasha where we stayed with a bunch of her relatives who lived on what she called "the good side of the tracks." Everybody bathed, everybody wore clean clothes, and the whole family ate together. There was Auntie Ophelia, Uncle Sylvester, Auntie Jessica, and numerous cousins. This is where Walter and I learned about table manners.

We were sitting at the table one evening—just smacking and chomping away because that home cooking tasted so good! All of a sudden, something told me that someone was staring. I looked up from my plate and saw that the whole family had stopped eating to stare at us. Walter was still smacking away, his head almost buried in the center of his plate.

I punched him in the side to get his attention. He looked up and stopped chewing in the middle of a mouthful.

"Eddie Gerald, you and Walter . . . well, there's a way of eating your food without your mouths being open so you don't have to make all those sounds," Auntie Ophelia offered graciously. Then she proceeded to demonstrate her delicate method of eating, while the rest of the family continued their meal.

She also taught us that the table was not an elbow rest, nor was it polite to pick your teeth or any other part of the body at the table. "Excuse me, please" was the password for escape, but it only worked if your plate was empty when you said it. From then on, we practiced eating every night with Auntie Ophelia coaching our every bite.

I loved the going and coming portion of our vacations, but I hated the staying—almost as much as I hated driving through Dallas.

———◆———

The sacks of sugar and yeast dwindled steadily in Grandma's little house, and Mama was looking for ways to expand her business. Evidently she found some, because the shelves in the kitchen began to bulge with factory-made bottles identified by fancy printed labels. Nobody ever delivered this new inventory—it just seemed to appear from nowhere.

Mama surprised me one day by announcing it was time for me to have a car. She knew I was a good driver, having "taught" me in Dallas. I preferred a motorcycle—a bright shiny red one—but she won since she was buying. She bought me a brown, four-door '54 Ford, which I promptly named "Honey Boy."

It wasn't long before I found out how whiskey bottles made it to our kitchen. "Honey Boy" was designated as the new pipeline. Mama sent me across the border into Wichita Falls, Texas, to pick up her "personal supply" of booze.

Every couple of weeks, I gathered my buddies and off we'd go on the 100-mile round trip. We looked like a normal bunch of kids looking for fun on a hot summer day. I suspected our mission was less than innocent. I didn't like being involved in the business at all, but I figured cruising anonymously to Texas and back was better than dipping, capping, and stacking chock.

One afternoon, we were at the Lawton city limits with a load of whiskey and rum in "Honey Boy's" trunk. I saw Mama's car barreling towards us, her arm frantically waving out the car window. I pulled over to the shoulder of the highway and waited for her to get stopped. I knew something was terribly wrong when she hoisted herself out of the car and ran towards us, her house shoes flip-flapping on the bubbly black top. Sweat beaded around her fat cheeks and trickled down her neck.

"You boys pile outta that car and get in mine, quick!" she yelled, waving her arms high over her head as if she were shooing chickens out of a garden. "The law's done caught on to this haul, and they're liable to be comin' any minute!"

Well, it didn't take our eight gangly legs very long to hit the asphalt and bolt for her car.

"Y'all go hang out at the Dairy Queen for 'bout an hour," she ordered from across the highway, "then Eddie Gerald, you get on home!!" Mama squeezed under "Honey Boy's" steering wheel, U-turned, and peeled rubber as she headed away from Lawton.

Calvin and Michael were pretty quiet on the way to the Dairy Queen although they swore to keep the afternoon's event a secret. It was the first time I had to fake being hungry, but I ordered a hamburger anyway. Calvin and Michael ordered cherry Cokes, guzzled them quickly, and said they wanted to walk home rather than wait on me to finish my burger.

When I finally got home, "Honey Boy" was parked in his usual place in the driveway and Mama was stocking the Coke machine as if nothing had happened. I went straight to my room and slammed the door.

I hated the business more than ever after that scare. What if *all* my friends found out? What if the school found out? What if the coaches found out? What if I got caught next time? What if I was destined to follow in Grandma's and Mama's footsteps?

6

JUNIOR JOCK

As usual, "Honey Boy" was polished to perfection as we rolled into the parking lot at Lawton High School. My black leather sax case added a look of class to the inside of the car, and my shirt crackled with starch as I reached for the tower of textbooks on the seat beside me. It felt good to get back to a routine after the unpredictable summer had vanished.

It was my first year at high school, and my 16-year-old brain automatically flirted with the fear of the unknown. I wondered if I would make the basketball team. What would I do if I didn't make it? Which teachers would I get? Would they be nice and helpful, or would they be ogres? Would the other kids like me? Would I be able to get the schedule I wanted? The list of fearsome questions about the future was endless.

Two things were certain though, and attaining them would keep me busy—I had to get C's or better if I wanted to stay in sports all year, and I had to stay in sports if I wanted to go to college.

During the first few weeks, I was busy surviving the tryouts for basketball, baseball, and track. After I was selected to be on each team, my thoughts turned to earning the school's Wolverine mascot emblem for my letter jacket. This jacket was much more special than an ordinary coat. It was a symbol of leadership, commitment, loyalty, and hard work.

The Wolverine patch was a sign of athletic achievement. These patches were awarded to the athletes at the end of each year in an all-school assembly. The coveted emblem would add an almost sacred stamp of approval, not only to the jacket, but to the person who wore it.

During sophomore orientation, I had learned about Wolverines. A wolverine is one of the most feared and respected members of the weasel family. It generally lives a solitary life in northern forests and stays alive by eating other animals. The wolverine is blackish in color with a light brown band on each side of its body, and is known primarily for its incredible strength. I promised myself that I would live up to our namesake.

The Lawton High School Wolverines had won State Champion for football two years in a row. It was obvious to me from the very beginning that the coaches, students, players, parents, teachers, and school board all wanted winning teams as badly as I did. What I wanted most of all was an opportunity to do my part in making that happen.

Football was out of the question my sophomore year since I was enrolled in band class. Nevertheless, I intended to earn a letter for each of the other sports: basketball, baseball, and track.

My best friend Byron and I had a lot in common. We both were in band class instead of on the football team. He played trombone and had already earned the honor of "first chair."

Not only did I envy his musical abilities, I literally had to look up to him. He was much taller than me and he quickly became my idol. He was smart, popular, good looking, and talented. The girls seemed to flock around him, so I constantly watched what he did and listened to what he said in their presence. My secret desire was to be pleasantly mobbed by some of his adoring females.

Two weeks after school started, I sauntered into band class as usual; got out my sax to warm up; and looked around the crowded room for Byron. His chair was empty and his music stand was blank.

"Where's Byron?" I shouted to anyone who could hear me over the ungodly noise of the warm-up drills.

Somebody hollered out, "He's gone to play football—he won't be in band anymore!"

Well, in less than twenty-four hours, I decided that if I continued to play in the band, I might be labeled a sissy, and I knew I was tougher than Byron. I had seen him play football in phys-ed, and I knew that I had more endur-ance, speed, and coordination than he did. It was time to take the sport kinda serious!

The next day, I was in the school office cancelling band and arranging for a late football tryout. Not only was the dream of a scholarship at stake, but so was my masculin-ity, or so it appeared.

The coaching staff accepted me for the football team and, sure enough, it got serious! The competition was fierce among my teammates and among the teams within our league. Oklahoma schools were well known for their athletic accomplishments, and I soon discovered how they earned so many titles.

Even though the coaches hinted that I had some of the qualities that make good athletes—quickness, flexibility, and determination—I spent a lot of time on the bench dur-ing my sophomore year. It was so frustrating to hear the coaches tell each other, "He's a natural," and then send in some other player! I worked my tail off to be better than the next guy. Get to practice early! Be the last to leave! Run faster! Jump higher! I learned early that a second ef-fort wasn't good enough—it was the third, fourth, and fifth one that made a difference.

The coaches had inherited the theory that in order to prove you really had guts, you had to run over a guy. Nobody asked my opinion, but I wanted to prove that using my brain could accomplish the same results. I tried to explain this to the coach: "Coach, it doesn't make much sense for me to run over this guy when I know that I can outrun him, outmaneuver him, leap over him, fake him out, or go over his head. So why should I try to run over him?" I had asked intelligently. Like I said, I spent a lot of time on the bench that year.

Football practices were both grueling and exhilarating. Often, I ran down the field with fear in my heart, but most of the time, I laughed as I ran. It was very exciting to run into a group of people who were running towards me. I knew they thought that because I was a newcomer, I was going to stand there like some idiot and let them cream me. I simply moved left or right or backwards and laughed to myself when they missed me. The coaches kept saying, "He just doesn't have any guts." I knew better, and after I saw guys get knocked out (not to mention the broken ribs and torn ligaments) I decided that running over someone was not the fun part. At least it wasn't fun for me.

———◆———

The Wolverines were consistent winners all through my sophomore and junior year. Each game that I was allowed to play added to my self-confidence. Each time I sat on the bench only added to my determination.

My senior year, however, was plagued by injuries. During the second game of the season, an opposing player hit me from the blind side and extended the ligaments in my leg. It was extremely painful and required extra care if I wanted to be able to play the rest of the season. So I began the process so familiar to athletes. I smeared liniment on the leg, warmed it with a vibrator, and wrapped it carefully before I played.

I had been taught that a good player just lives with pain and plays anyway. Injuries could not interfere. I also knew the college scouts were watching every high school game throughout the country, hoping to find seniors with superstar potential. I prayed fervently for a speedy recovery!

My leg felt good for the final game of the season, which was with our number one rival—Duncan, Oklahoma. I desperately wanted to end my high school football career with some fancy break-aways and at least one touchdown. However, my hopes were wiped out in an instant of anguish.

On one of the early plays of the game, I had to leap over a fallen player to avoid a penalty, and he grabbed my leg as I went. I managed to stay upright for about two seconds, then the leg just went limp. The bench was my home until halftime, but I was determined to play the second half.

In the locker room, I went through the same procedure of smearings and wrappings; but when it was time to go back in the game, the leg would not go. When the coach heard, he came to me on the bench and said, "You let my team down."

I couldn't believe it. I couldn't believe he said that. Disbelief turned quickly to rage, and I yelled at him what I instinctively knew: "Do you realize that if I go out there on this leg, I may not have a future in college or the rest of my life? *I cannot play!*"

The coach's face registered nothing as he turned back to the sideline to watch the second half kickoff.

The final score of that game was 0–0, yet I got the dirtiest looks in the world from my teammates. What hurt, even more than the injury itself, was that the coach I had played for all through high school treated me like a traitor.

I guess it didn't matter that I had lettered two years in football, track, and basketball. Obviously, it was no longer important that I had set the school record of 19.2 in low hurdles, and the State Low Hurdles Championship had my name on it. No one seemed to remember that I was All-State Halfback and led in rushing and scoring. I received the league's Player-of-the-Year Award, and my peers selected me as tops in leadership, achievement, service, and personality. Should these honors have gone to someone else? A four-year scholarship to the University of Oklahoma was mine if I accepted it, and the coach says, "You let my team down!" That's when I realized I was playing only for myself.

———◆———

I was scheduled to go to O.U. the next day for a pre-entrance interview with the coaching staff. I wrapped my leg again and went on crutches, trying to hide the wound in my heart. While I was there, they x-rayed my leg and the doctor told me in no uncertain terms: "If you had gone out and got this leg hit one more time, you'd probably be on crutches the rest of your life. I'm not going to operate on it; you just have to stay off of it."

———◆———

After returning from the O.U. visit, I searched the Lawton newspaper for reports of that final, dismal game. My leg started feeling better as I read about the awards I had been given, but then I came to a paragraph that stunned me. One of the coaches was quoted as saying, "Eddie is a good all-around athlete and probably could have been great if he had specialized in any one sport. . . ."

I didn't realize it at the time, but the coach's summary of me provided the incentive I was going to need to fulfill my life's goals. I wish I had been wise enough to thank him for his honesty.

———◆———

Things had changed drastically at home and I couldn't wait to escape. Here I was, 18 years old, getting ready to start college in the fall, and Mama presented Walter and me with a baby brother. It was embarrassing for some reason—maybe because I was the last to know. Her obesity had hidden the fact of her pregnancy.

I should have figured out that something was going on. Her women friends had been calling her "Big Girl" instead of Geraldine, and they had joked about my dad's previous visit. After Reggie was born, Mama's nickname stuck, and even I called her Big Girl from then on.

After considering numerous offers from colleges all over the United States, I decided to stay on Oklahoma turf to get my college degree. One of my happiest moments was signing a letter of intent to attend the University of Oklahoma, home of The Big Red Sooners.

Big Girl attended the signing ceremony with me, but Dad, as usual, was absent. She was openly proud that I had been given a full athletic scholarship to a school so close to home.

The day after I graduated from high school in 1965, I moved to Oklahoma City and checked into the YMCA. It was just the beginning of my personal declaration of independence.

7

PIGSKIN POLKA

The Sooner freshman ballplayers were on hold for a year, unless they were able to make the varsity team. This rarely happened, and I began to kid my teammates about the name "Sooners." I told them it came from the first freshman O.U. player who kept telling himself, "Sooner or later, I'm gonna make it." In actuality, it was handed down from the early days of Oklahoma's history. "Sooner" was the nickname given to the early settlers who invaded Oklahoma's Indian territory in hopes of claiming unassigned acreage during the land-boom of the late 1800's. Also known as "Boomers," the two terms were frequently combined.

At any rate, I knew that sooner or later, *I* was going to make it. But in the meantime, it was block, tackle, catch the ball; block, tackle, catch the ball. I would often daydream during practices to relieve the boredom of the repetitious "basics." I had had excellent coaches in high school, and I was certain that they had taught me everything there was to know about football.

Meetings were even worse. Sleeping while the coaches talked was a no-no, but I could not stay awake if I sat still for more than two minutes! The coaches yelled at me frequently: "Hinton, you'll never make the varsity! You're not paying attention! You'll never make it!"

Like I said, playing time for freshmen was rare, but occasionally, they'd put me in an exhibition game. I knew what to do. I'd score some touchdowns and gain the most yardage. The coaches kept saying, "You don't do this," and "You don't do that," and all I cared about was getting in the game! From my point of view, winning or losing wasn't the point, although I knew I would be judged by the points I scored or failed to score. To me, the point of it all was about being in the game. I knew if I played my very best, everything else would work out perfectly.

At the beginning of my sophomore year, O.U. enlisted some new coaches. Jim MacKenzie was the new head man, and he gave us second-stringers the chance we'd all been waiting for.

"I don't care if you are on the varsity, first team, or second team! You are all going to start together on the bottom line and work for a position!" MacKenzie had decreed on the first day of his reign.

Hallelujah, brother! I thought gleefully. *Just give me the opportunity to show you what I can do!* My fervent hope was that no one had told him about my occasional naps.

———◆———

What was to be the greatest excitement of my college career washed over me the very first time I trotted onto Owen Field at Oklahoma's Memorial Stadium. The applause of 51,000 enthusiastic football fans reverberated through my helmet, and chill bumps popped out all over my body. I knew I was part of something really special.

It was an honor and a privilege to wear the crimson and cream varsity uniform. Of all the threads I had in my closet, this uniform made me feel the best! If you had on that jersey, you *were* somebody. I felt like I had earned the privilege of wearing it, simply because I had survived Coach MacKenzie's rigorous tryouts. Now it was up to me to keep from losing my shirt.

The Sooners were playing Oregon, and we only had a meager 23 yards rushing and 43 passing after a flat first half. I was elected punt returner to open the second half, and my job was to catch the ball on the opening kick off.

There were at least 21 obstacles between me and scoring. Not only did I have to avoid the 11 charging opponents, I had to make sure I didn't collide with the 10 allies who were charging at the chargers.

My first collegiate game. My first real action. My first punt return. The spiraling ball met me at the 37-yard line. I zigged a little bit, then shifted myself into overdrive and followed the sideline toward the goal. A quick glance over my shoulder confirmed that my teammates had done their job. It was amazing—there was no one even close! It was immediately obvious that nobody could catch me. I became so relaxed and so smug at the thought of scoring a touchdown that I didn't even feel the ball slide out of my hands. All of a sudden, there it was, floating towards the sideline. The ball could have bounced out of bounds, but for some blessed reason, it bounced right back into my hands and I didn't even break stride! I ran into the end zone, chalking up 63 yards and 6 glorious points while my heart threatened to burst from my heaving chest! *Scared???* It felt like my body would overdose on its own adrenalin!

The fans screamed and hollered in exultation as I breathlessly made my way to the bench, grinning from ear to ear. I was *so* thankful that the ball had recovered itself, and had saved me from the excruciating embarrassment of a dropped ball. My teammates welcomed me at the sideline with exuberant hugs and congratulatory smacks on the rump. Coach MacKenzie, I noticed, was looking at me with a mixture of appreciation and disdain. "Uh, Eddie," he said, sideling closer, "let's quit clowning around, okay?" he urged with sarcasm.

I was flabbergasted. *"CLOWNING?"* I gasped in disbelief, *"I wasn't clowning! I could have made the biggest fool out of myself. . . ."* My attempts to explain were cut short, for he had already turned around to watch the point-after attempt.

Fortunately, by the end of the game, I was considered a hero; and miraculously, by the end of that season, I led the nation in punt returns. I had to prove to someone that I hadn't been clowning around.

———◆———

By the beginning of my junior year, my statistics and reputation spoke for themselves. My freshman days were far behind me, and I started looking to the future.

One afternoon, I was studying our football schedule for the next season, which would be my final year at O.U., and the Notre Dame game practically jumped off the page at me. A brilliant idea started swirling in my head.

According to the schedule, formidable Notre Dame would be our first opponent of the season. The game would be nationally televised, which meant that professional football scouts would be watching. I was smart enough to know that if I played an exceptional game, or at least scored a long touchdown, the chances were real good that I'd get picked for the pros. But I wanted a clincher big play that would make me and the whole team look good, and even take the fans by surprise. The play began to emerge in my thoughts, and once I was sure of it, I decided to approach the subject with Barry Switzer, our Offensive Coordinator.

We were walking off the practice field one morning and he had just finished complimenting me on my performance during pattern drills. The moment was perfect. I casually mentioned next year's schedule, hoping to impress him with my foresight. "Yup," I said wistfully, "if we can just get past that opening game with Notre Dame next year, we oughta have a great season."

He mumbled something about next *week's* game, but I went further, unwilling to be sidetracked.

"Coach, you know that little pass we have," I began, "that look-in pass where I come off the line three yards and veer in at a 45-degree angle and go back into all the traffic between safeties and linebackers?" I paused questioningly, waiting for his go-ahead. He knew exactly which play I was talking about, so I continued more confidently: "Well, if Bobby can raise up and throw the ball to me the moment I come off the line; and if I can veer in on a perfect stride; and if he can throw the ball where I don't have to reach for it or stretch for it or wait on it, I can score," I said matter-of-factly.

I had captured his attention and proceeded to the most important element of the play—the element of surprise. "We have to throw it on the first down—the first play of the game," I advised urgently. "It'll catch them completely off guard . . . catch the whole *nation* off guard," I said excitedly.

Coach Switzer said, "What?? Say that again."

We had stopped in the shade of the stadium fence and I explained it again. I borrowed his clipboard and drew a diagram of exactly where Bobby Warmack, our quarterback, should be when he threw the ball, and exactly where I needed to be to catch it. He agreed to discuss the play with Coach Fairbanks and came back to me the next day with an approval.

That whole spring training and most of the summer, Bobby and I were dedicated to practicing just that one

play. It had to be perfect. When I made my cut, I could not
be stumbling. Bobby's pass had to be right on target. My
job was to run between the Notre Dame defenders and
leave them wondering what happened.

———◆———

It was a perfect day for football and we had a perfect
surprise for Notre Dame and the nation. The television
cameras were rolling, the faithful fans were rocking the
bleachers with their enthusiastic support, and Bobby was
calling the snap. The play was beautifully timed, as we all
knew it would be.

When I got back to the sideline from the end zone, I was
beyond happiness.

"That play is not designed to score, Eddie," Switzer
said, slapping my helmet joyfully. "How did you know?
How did you know it would work?" he questioned insistently.

"Oh, I don't know, Coach," I grinned modestly. "Just a
feelin' deep down, I guess. Maybe I'm psychic!" I offered, jokingly.

"Maybe you're just a natural show-off, too!" he
laughed, "but the main thing is, it worked! We'd both be
in hot water if it hadn't!"

His casual comment set me to thinking, and I suddenly
realized that coaches had bosses, too. They had to perform just like the players, only at a different level of
"team." He had taken the risk with me. He had possibly
put his job on the line. He had trusted me. My renewed
respect for the man and his position made my eyes water.

Notre Dame, undaunted by our shrewdness, did not let
up on us. So what was I going to do for the rest of the
game? I hadn't planned an encore; but I figured the more
flexibility I could show in this game, the more valuable

I'd look to the scouts. So I came up with another bright idea.

I hadn't played defense since high school, but I knew I could guard Notre Dame's All American split end, Jim Seymour, a towering 6′4″ player with a long stride and great coordination. He was outmaneuvering our man, so it seemed like the risk involved would be worth a try.

"Coach, I can guard Seymour," I stated positively. "If he runs back, I can outrun him. If he catches the ball, I'll go catch him. He won't get past me," I promised.

Since I had proven myself on the first play of the game, Coach Switzer shrugged and said, "Well, what have we got to lose?"

Into the game I went, but now I had to react from a defensive point of view. When Seymour lined up across from me, Notre Dame's quarterback, Terry Hanratty looked over his center at me and said with astonishment, "What the . . . he's not . . . what is this . . ." and called time out.

The Notre Dame team went to the sideline. They came back to the line of scrimmage and called a couple of plays, but Hanratty wouldn't throw to Seymour. Finally they had to test me.

I knew the ball was coming my way because Seymour came at me the instant the ball was snapped. I could tell he was determined, and much to my disgust, I slipped and almost fell. He curled to the right and caught the ball. Well, that made me angry because I had given my word that he would not get past me. So I ran in front of him, ripped the ball out of his hands, and ran back 32 yards. That play set up our next touchdown and eventually the half ended at 14-0.

In the locker room, I took Coach Switzer aside and told him straight out, "I'm worn slick! I ain't never played offense and defense in the same game before," I confessed.

"I'm through with that scene! Just put me back where I belong!"

The second half was uneventful for me, as Notre Dame's offense dominated the game. The legendary Fighting Irish concluded their Oklahoma invasion by trouncing us, 45-21. I'd sooner have won; but, as I was to find out later, I accomplished what I had set out to do. That game counted *big* toward a possible pro career.

RING AROUND THE R.O.T.C.

In addition to academics and sports, I had enrolled in the Reserve Officer Training Corps (R.O.T.C.) as a freshman at the University of Oklahoma, along with the other athletes. I was gungho about the Army's program until the end of my sophomore year. Then I realized that my commitment to R.O.T.C. would keep me from playing pro ball, *if* I got the opportunity to do so, because the cadets were expected to serve as commissioned officers after graduation.

I started looking for ways to fulfill my military obligation without being in the R.O.T.C. program. A plan began to emerge: I could attend the '68 Fall semester and finish my senior year football season; then, instead of enrolling in the '69 Spring semester, drop out of school; join the National Guard; and go to boot camp for four and a half months. If all that worked according to plan, I'd know the results of the pro sports draft before boot camp started. After boot camp, I'd be eligible to go play pro ball for the '69 season, return to school in January of '70 and graduate in May of '70. Simple, or so I thought.

I may have been the low-hurdles champ from Lawton High School, but I'd never faced an obstacle like this before. My objective was to sell the school and the military authorities on my plan.

————◆————

"You can't do that, Hinton! You can't just drop out of R.O.T.C.!" the athletic director had said.

"Let me explain it to you again, sir. I want to play pro ball—I do not want to go into the Army from R.O.T.C. I will fulfill my military obligation in the National Guard for six years." I outlined my plan fully for the dean of men.

"But the rules say, Hinton, you can't . . ."

"Let me explain it to you again, sir. I want to play pro ball. . . ." I told him politely.

"You don't even know if you'll have the option to play with the pros. You're only a sophomore! That's two years away," the R.O.T.C. commanding officer had protested.

"Sirs, may I explain it to you again? I want to play pro ball. . . ." I was exasperated by all the delays, but unwilling to give up.

On and on it went—up the lines of authority; over the chains of command; in and through the offices and in-baskets of the official experts who were trying to tell me how to live my life.

I knew I was making progress when they reluctantly helped me by pointing out obstacles I had not foreseen. I would have to go to summer school to get the seven extra credits to make the plan work; and "Of course," they reminded me dolefully, "you won't be graduating with your class."

I thought the matter got handled, because I never got a definite "No" from anybody.

Then, during sign-up week for my junior hours, I was again called before the athletic director, the president of the university, the dean of men, and the commanding officer of the R.O.T.C. program. They couldn't figure out what was going on and I assured them I didn't know either. As far as I was concerned, I was just trying to plan my future. The meeting was a rerun of all the others, except that it had expanded to include life after football.

"I don't want to be in the Army—I'm gonna play professional football. When I'm through playin' pro ball, I'm goin' into business for myself. That's why I signed up for business administration classes," I explained methodically.

"Do you know what chances you might have to play pro ball out of the thousands of colleges and the hundreds of thousands of athletes competing to be chosen? What are your odds? What about your health? You may not be able to play. . . ."

"I'm not worried about all that," I assured the group of distinguished authority figures. "What I want to do is be the best possible athlete I can be. I figure the rest of it will take care of itself," I concluded honestly.

Finally I managed to convince them. It could be done, *but* I had to pick a different major course of study. The business classes I had selected interfered with football practice.

The dean of men suggested a major in liberal arts or education, so I chose special education. If I couldn't do what I needed and wanted to do, maybe I could work with people and help them in some way. Educating myself for the business world would have to wait.

9

THE LAST TO KNOW

The Oklahoma Sooners tied the Kansas State Wildcats for the prized Big Eight Conference Crown. That meant our team would play against Southern Methodist University in the Astro-Bluebonnet Bowl on New Year's Eve, 1968. Normally, I would have been thrilled to participate in such a celebrated event, particularly since we would be playing in the newly constructed and world famous Astrodome in Houston. However, Bobby Warmack and I had been invited as individual players to participate in the Hula Bowl in Honolulu, Hawaii at the same time. For about two seconds, I was torn between "Howdy" and "Aloha." Then I realized—we didn't have an honorable choice. We would follow the crimson and cream colors all the way to the Gulf and play our last college game under the "Dome."

It was a dreadful game, to say the least. Apparently, our hearts were just not in it. All I could envision were cheerleaders in hula skirts. Our team missed a field goal in the final seconds of the game, and S.M.U. squeaked past us, 28–27. Nothing went right. Warmack got his first major injury during this final, farewell salute. It was a bummer all the way around and, ironically, it was a bummer time in my life.

The fall semester was over and I would not be returning for the Spring session in '69. Uncle Sam and his National Guard were waiting for me. During the year, I had given a speech about staying in school to the kids at Douglass Junior High. Here I was, about to become a dropout myself. Although I knew I'd be back to get my degree, I felt like a hypocrite.

The entire month of January, I was in total limbo and thoroughly lost. I had just returned to the O.U. campus after spending the Christmas holidays in Lawton with Big Girl, Walter, and Reggie.

There were no classes for me. There were no practices. There were no phone calls—yet. Waiting on the professional football draft was my only activity. In a few short days, I would be leaving for National Guard boot camp at Ft. Polk, Louisiana. I would be leaving my whole life behind.

The television in my dorm room was my link to the outside world while I waited like an expectant father for some good news. I watched the New York Jets beat the Baltimore Colts in Super Bowl III and kept wondering if I would be picked by any of the major teams, or if it would be some weakling team in the fourth or fifth round. The AFL and the NFL were both active and competitive in the draft, so I was relatively certain I'd be chosen by *somebody* before it was all over.

Late one evening I got a perplexing phone call from a guy who said he was a sports editor or something. He talked so fast, I could hardly understand him.

"Congratulations, Eddie! Have you heard the good news?" he asked excitedly.

"What good news?" I asked curiously.

"You got drafted Number One by Baltimore!" he exclaimed happily.

I said, "Look, buster, thanks anyway, but I'm expecting a very important phone call . . . I don't have time for pranks, okay?"

"I'm serious!" he said. "You got drafted Number One by the Baltimore Colts!"

"Yeah, right!" I said flatly, even more skeptical than before. The nerve of this guy! "If I got drafted, how come they didn't call me?" I didn't wait for an answer. I was getting angrier by the second. "I don't have time to . . . you're tying up my line and I'm waitin' for an important phone call," I accused severely.

"What am I going to have to do to convince you?" he shrieked in total frustration. "You're Baltimore's Number One Draft choice!"

"Wait a minute," I ordered. "Are you saying that this is the same team that just played in the Super Bowl? Is this the same team that just played in the Super Bowl against the Jets?" I quizzed thoroughly.

He said, "Yep . . . yeah, that's the team!"

". . . the team that Johnny Unitas plays on?" I insisted, trying to keep from punching him through the phone. This guy just didn't know when to quit!

"Yeah!" he confirmed with relief. "Yeah! You got it!" he said with approval.

I cursed under my breath and slammed the receiver down in its cradle! What a sense of humor that creep had. I hadn't seen anything in print or on the television, nor had there been any phone calls during the day, except for this joker. "The jerk! Tying up my line!" I mumbled disgustedly.

A few days later, I gave up my dorm room, packed my duffel bag, told my closest friends good-bye, and surrendered myself to the Greyhound Bus Company in Oklahoma City. Boot camp, here I come. The thought of it made me nauseous. There still had been no word regarding the draft.

I could not imagine why I hadn't been picked for the pros. By this time, *any* team would have been okay with me. It was a lonely, dismal bus ride from the Land of the Big Red Sooners.

When the bus stopped in Houston to pick up more passengers, I wandered into the terminal for a pit stop and a hot dog. On the way back to the bus with both hands full of food, I happened to pass a newspaper vending machine. Imagine my surprise when I saw a familiar name in the headlines! **Eddie Hinton, Picked Number One By Baltimore!**

The bus was loading as I tried to juggle the snacks and dig in my pockets for a quarter at the same time. I could hardly wait to read about my future! The questions hammered in my head: Why didn't they call me? How come I hadn't seen it on TV? Why was I the last one to know? What should I do now? I couldn't believe that Baltimore hadn't called me, and here I was on my way to four and a half months of boot camp!

I must have read the article hundreds of times between Houston and Ft. Polk. It seemed like we got there in no time at all.

10

WISH LISTS ARE NEGOTIABLE

It was very humbling to go from campus football hero to Ft. Polk's kitchen patrol. For weeks, I experienced a personal and cultural shock for which I was not prepared. The simple things in life suddenly took on new meaning. Food. Privacy. Telephones. Women. Television. Hair. Wardrobe. Transportation. Rights. There were limited amounts of these "luxuries" in my new environment, if they happened to be available at all.

I suffered telephone withdrawal symptoms. My skin yearned for a colorful silk shirt. I dreamed of delicious, delectable morsels. I kept asking myself, *Can a pro football career possibly be worth going through all this torture?*

Just about the time I adjusted to military existence, I received the long-awaited letter from the Colts. It hadn't occurred to me that they might have had trouble locating my whereabouts. Their instructions were for me to contact their office as soon as I was "out" so we could proceed with contract negotiations. The letter reminded me that there was a future "out there"—that everything in life is temporary.

———◆———

Back home, I didn't know who to turn to for help with my contract, but I knew what the process was all about: someone offers you something and you offer them something and then it's a matter of compromise. After my boot camp experiences at Ft. Polk, I felt like I could handle anything. But just to be ahead of the game, I checked with someone who'd been there before me.

I called a friend of mine who played for the Dallas Cowboys, and he put me in touch with a man in Dallas who could possibly help me. Well, the guy sounded real good on the phone and he told me he was going to be on the East Coast about the same time I was going to Baltimore. To save on time and travel expenses, I arranged to meet Mr. Franklin at the Colts' office on the appointed day.

I was already visiting with Steve Rosenbloom, Manager of the Colts, when my "advisor" was ushered to an adjacent chair. Our conversation rapidly made its way to the contract. When Mr. Rosenbloom offered us a figure, Mr. Franklin turned to me and said, "That's a lot of money, Eddie!" with an overabundance of awe in his voice.

Just the way he said it made me want to gag. I said to myself, *This guy's got to be crazy! He must mean, That's a lot of money for a little black kid that's comin' up!* But it wasn't a lot of money according to my research. My intuition told me Mr. Franklin and I were destined for doom. There was no way to surmount the gulf that existed between our experiences and our expectations. It was a mistake not to have met him prior to the meeting. *Might as well get this over with now,* I thought to myself, ignoring the bile that threatened to rise in my throat.

"Mr. Rosenbloom, would you mind excusin' us for about five minutes?" I requested politely. "I need to bring Mr. Franklin up to date on a couple of matters."

"Sure," he said warmly. "You two go ahead and visit, while I check with my secretary on tomorrow's schedule. Just holler when you're ready," he said as he left the room, throwing us strange looks on his way out.

The door of the office closed gently; I stood up and began to pace in front of Mr. Franklin.

"Mr. Franklin," I began candidly, "it looks like we have a serious communication gap. Probably the best thing for you to do is go catch that plane you flew in on and go back to Dallas," I said, as if I were giving him directions to the men's room. "Send me a bill for any extra expenses you may have incurred. I'll proceed from here on my own. Thank you for your time."

He tried to explain why I needed him, but none of his reasons were meaningful. There was no way to save this situation, so I thanked him rather halfheartedly for his concern and opened the door. He got the message and left, leaving me to explain his sudden absence to Mr. Rosenbloom.

When Mr. Rosenbloom came back in the room, I apologized for any inconvenience the meeting had caused him. I informed him that I had to go back to Oklahoma and massage some figures; and that I'd be back in touch with him soon.

If there *was* a next meeting, I vowed to attend it alone. If there were going to be any mistakes made, I wanted them to be Eddie Hinton's. That's the only way I knew to learn about life.

———◆———

Common sense told me I couldn't verbally negotiate with the high-powered business man, but one thing I *could* do was type. I made a list of everything I wanted—the salary, the bonuses, the "if" clauses—and I made several copies. I wasn't greedy, but I had a fair idea of my value. I'd let the paper do the talking.

When my list was complete, I called Mr. Rosenbloom. He arranged for the Colts to fly me from Oklahoma to Baltimore again. After my arrival and the standard ritualized chitchat, Mr. Rosenbloom started telling me again what the Colts had to offer.

"Well, you know, Mr. Rosenbloom," I ventured, "I don't know how to talk business with y'all and I don't know much about negotiatin', but this is what I want." I pulled out my typewritten list and placed it on his desk as if it were the Magna Charta.

He took the slightly crumpled "wish list" in both hands and began to study it.

His body language was not good. "This is totally absurd," his face said, but I sat motionless and waited for him to finish.

"Well, sir, do you agree?" I asked nonchalantly.

Of course he said no and attempted to proceed with the negotiations. The forgotten list contained everything I wanted, so I figured it was time for me to leave. I no longer had any business to discuss. I politely interrupted Mr. Rosenbloom's discourse. "Sir, would you do me a favor?" I asked softly.

"Well, sure if I can," he agreed tersely. "What is it?"

I hid the tremors, looked him straight in the eye and said, "Would you please ask your secretary to find out what time the next plane is goin' back to Oklahoma?"

———◆———

Two times up—two times back. Mr. Rosenbloom assured me they would call after they "massaged" my list and reached a decision.

His answer made me want to whoop and holler. "Don't come up here—we accept. We'll send *you* the contract!"

I may not have much polish, but I do get to the point.

11

CRACKED WEDDING BELLS

Big Girl was an ever-present power in my life. Her inner strength was both a blessing and a curse to me—sometimes it was uplifting and sometimes it was oppressive. As a general rule, I just stayed out of her way.

I learned early that women were to be feared, respected, obeyed, accommodated, anticipated, manipulated, and worshiped. I also learned early not to trust them. My limited experiences indicated that they were totally unpredictable. My adoption of this opinion came through painful and embarrassing circumstances.

There was a girl in my fourth grade class who was teased by everyone about being so large. She was taller than any of the other girls and deserved a trophy for "class chunky." We all called her "Big Louise," and cruelly took advantage of every opportunity to ridicule her.

One day I passed her desk on the way to the pencil sharpener, exploiting the fact that Mrs. Jacobs, our teacher, was out of the room momentarily. Big Louise was stuffing some textbooks into the storage space under her seat and I leaned across the desk top to launch my verbal attack.

"Big Louise. Big Louise. Bigger than me, even on her knees," I jeered nastily.

Well, she also took advantage of Mrs. Jacobs' absence
by raising up from her crouched position and slapping the
heck out of me—knocked me over the desk behind hers,
scattering its contents everywhere! Of course, the teacher
walked back into the room just as I was picking myself up
off the floor.

I didn't have time to recover from the shock of Big
Louise's counter attack. Mrs. Jacobs held a quick trial and
acted as both judge and jury. She promptly sentenced me
to a paddling in front of the class, and from then on, I kept
my distance from females of all sizes, shapes, and colors.

Ironically, I was most comfortable around women, even
though I didn't want to get too close to them. I knew I
could not enter the sanctity of their illusive domain. Big
Girl's demeanor had always seemed to impart "No Men
Allowed," and I figured that applied to me.

There were no male role models, so I had had to de-
velop my own unique style of masculinity. Daddy wasn't
around enough to be an "example"; Walter was too young
to be one; and I knew I didn't want to be like the men who
came to Geraldine's Place.

There was very little time in my life for dating. However, it was important to me to give the impression that I
dated a lot. So whenever there were parties to attend, I
rounded up as many girls as I could peacefully handle and
escorted them to school events. Arriving at these parties
with an entourage of beautiful female companions established my image as a full-fledged man. Few people knew
how I really operated.

After making my desired entrance and enscouncing the
girls at the party, I would leave. There was always a back
door and I just quietly disappeared. I usually went home
or back to the dorm and studied or watched television for
a couple of hours. About the time the party was scheduled
to end, I returned via the same back door, picked up my
harem, and delivered them safely home. This scenario

seemed to work well for everyone involved, particularly for me the following day in the locker room.

The guys were in awe of my connived prowess and they made up the most delicious stories about my mysterious absence the night before. I didn't have to say a word, which also meant I didn't have to lie.

Watching television during the late '50's and early '60's gave me a rather distorted view of how life was supposed to be. I was particularly drawn to the "good life" commercials—you know, the ones where there's the Rolls Royce on the flagstone driveway in front of the Tudor English castle on the 500-acre wooded estate and the gentleman in the Italian-made suit is intimately assisting the beautiful blond in the mink coat into the back seat of the car. You know the one! Well, I wanted one of those—one of everything in the picture tube except the man. I always put *me* in his place.

During my junior year at O.U., I met Marcia, that beautiful, blond, wonderful, stimulating apparition that could have been in commercials. She was also a student at O.U. and a soon-to-be-divorced mother with a seven-year-old son named Barton. Marcia and Bart were carbon copies of each other—flaxen hair, blue eyes and Caucasian skin.

The three of us fell in love almost immediately. I always wanted the best of everything, and Marcia and Bart were it. Marcia finalized her divorce from Bart's father, and we continued to see each other discreetly for the next two years. My sense of completeness when I was with them overshadowed the complications that appeared as a result of our relationship.

I knew that the game of football was geared toward middle America, and in the late '60's, middle America was not ready for its football heroes to be interracially married. Neither were the promoters of pro sports, because players of mixed marriages were not marketable on or off the field. I didn't care about being "marketed" but I *did* want to play pro ball, so we kept our engagement a secret.

As soon as the hallowed Colts document could be signed—the very same day in fact—Marcia and I planned to be married. The wedding would have to be on the spur of the moment since it was entirely dependent on the delivery of the contract.

Marcia's parents were not informed of our wedding plans. Neither of us wanted to face any opposition whatsoever, and she assured me there would be some if they found out.

It was June 30, 1969. The contract arrived, we had our own signature party, and then we called the preacher. Just four days earlier, I had celebrated my twenty-second birthday; and here I was, taking on the role of professional athlete, husband, and father all on the same day.

We invited Big Girl by telephone to the hastily planned celebration, knowing that she would have time to make the hour-and-a-half drive from Lawton. I could tell she was very upset with me, but other than saying "Don't ever trust no white woman," she clammed up and I knew the conversation was over.

Big Girl didn't show up for the wedding, and her hasty admonition rang in my ears like cracked wedding bells.

After the "I do's" were exchanged, Marcia, Bart, and I returned to Marcia's house to spend our first night together as a family.

It was after 11:00 pm when the phone rang. The long-distance operator asked if I'd accept a collect call from the Lawton Police Department. I should have said no. Big Girl was in jail, and somebody had to go bail her out! Guess who got the job.

Needless to say, Marcia was livid!

"Why is she doing this, Eddie?" she raged. "This is our wedding night and it's wrong for her to expect you to leave tonight. I think she's just trying a power play," she accused intuitively.

"But, she's *my mother!*" I said, trying to reason with her. "She's in jail! There isn't anyone else who can get her out! How can you be so heartless?" I said, looking for sympathy in my dilemma.

Marcia started crying. Then I started crying. This frustrating situation was fueled by the buildup of tension from the day's momentous events.

Just a few hours earlier, we had completed our vows to love, honor, and cherish each other; and here we were, arguing and yelling already. I was dog-tired and torturously torn between the two women I loved. We were at an impasse, so I decided to get another vote on whether or not I should go bail Big Girl out.

Bart was not easily awakened, but when he showed signs of coherence, I presented my case.

"Bart, tell your mom," I began in partnership, ". . . wouldn't you help your mother if she was in trouble?" I prompted.

"Well . . . yeah, I guess I would," he replied, sensing the danger of taking sides so early in this new family game we were playing. Evidently, he was awake enough to make the connection between our red-rimmed eyes and the question I had posed.

"Mother, why were you and Eddie crying?" Bart asked abruptly. "I thought we married Eddie to make him happy!" he smiled innocently.

Marcia and I looked at each other and burst out laughing. Bart's youthful wisdom made us realize what a ridiculous situation we were in. The tension in the room vanished as she made her final statement regarding the whole mess. "Well, you go on," she said agreeably, "but I'm not going. I'll just wait here for you," she promised with *promise* in her voice.

I arrived in Lawton about one o'clock in the morning. Instead of going directly to the police station, I headed for Big Girl's house just to make sure everything was all right there. I had no idea why she was in jail—I hoped the place was still standing. Somebody could've torched it, for all I knew. I was both relieved and outraged when I drove in the driveway. There she was, sitting on the top step of the front porch. This time, Marcia's power-play comment bonged in my brain.

"'Zat you, Eddie Gerald?" Mama asked timidly, as I got out of the car and walked toward the porch. The only smoke I smelled was emanating from under my collar, so I surmised that she and the house were okay.

"Yeah, Big Girl, it's me," I answered shortly. "What you doin' home?" I demanded rudely. "I was just on my way to the police station—how did you get out?" I asked disgustedly.

"Well, the sergeant jus' came to the cell and said I could go this time, but not to never show up there again," she explained hastily. "I figgered you wasn't comin' anyway, so I didn't call you back," she added with an invisible sneer.

"This is my wedding night, Mama," I exploded. "I ought to be home with my new family and here I am in Lawton, Oklahoma, in the wee hours of this god-awful mornin' for nothin'!" I exclaimed with loathing.

Her eyes were barely visible. She stiffened and turned her hardened face away from my intense stare. This would get us nowhere, and I knew it was up to me to try to salvage our relationship.

"Why didn't you come?" I asked softly, recovering some of my composure.

She sat motionless and didn't answer. I suspected she *couldn't* answer my simplistic question, so I eased my weary body onto the rough planks beside her.

"You may not approve of the things I do, Mama; and you may not like Marcia. But the fact is, I'm married now." I paused to let her absorb the reality of it. "The fact is I'm married to a white woman with a white son and I love them both very much. Now you can either accept that or not," I said arbitrarily. "If you do, we'll all be one big happy family, and if you don't . . . well, we just won't come around to bother you."

There. It was said. The cord of bondage that linked us together was sheared in an instant.

Big Girl's head dipped closer to her lap. Barely discernible dark spots appeared on the bodice of her dress, but she didn't speak—couldn't speak.

"I'm leavin' for Baltimore next week, Mama, and I'll be up there a long time. I was hopin' you'd come see me play," I admitted openly.

She picked at an unseen snag in her dress and cleared her throat.

"Oh . . . well, ah . . . I ain't never been to Baltimore before . . . that ol' car of mine . . . don't know if it'd make it or not . . .," she replied hesitantly.

"I'll send you an airplane ticket and meet you at the airport," I promised. "We'll show you the town and I'll make a touchdown for you," I vowed solemnly.

She wiped her face with the back of her hand and pushed her bulk up off the porch. I stood too, towering over her even though I was on the bottom step.

"Eddie Gerald, I'm sorry for . . ."

"You don't need to apologize, Mama," I interrupted gently. "I just want you to know I still love you."

My arms had no trouble finding her in the darkness and for the first time ever, we held each other as friends.

12

SPRING TRAINING

After arriving at the Colts' training base in Maryland, I was shipped directly to Chicago to train for an exhibition game as a player for the Chicago College All-Star Team. This game was actually a professional football function and its purpose was to watch the country's newest and best rookie pros in action. Our ominous opponent was the World Champion New York Jets, and I'm proud to say, we certainly gave them a run for their money. New York barely topped us at 26–24. It was the closest All-Star game since 1936 when Detroit and the rookies tied at 7–7.

By the time I returned to the Colts' home base, I was a week behind the rest of the team. They had been practicing together every day getting ready for our opening exhibition game. I had to hustle to catch up, even though I had just come from playing the World Champs!

My performance was not impressive during the first half of the season. Like the fans, I expected Baltimore's first draft choice (yours truly) to step immediately into the lineup and become another Gale Sayers or Jim Brown.

In high school and college I played regularly and was generally acclaimed for my performance. It didn't take long to find out that things were different in the big time.

My job as a rookie was not to *play* football, but to observe football being played. This was quite a comedown for me after my active junior and senior seasons at O.U. It was back to the bench again.

I kept asking myself, *How in the world can I get good at this game if they don't let me play?* I knew I had more speed, more finesse, and more coordination than some of my counterparts. Besides that, I was bigger than most of the guys who were elbowing for a running/receiving position. My confidence began to slip away while I waited for a chance to prove myself.

Then a familiar voice within me said, *You need to set some goals, Eddie! You've been so busy getting here, you forgot to say what you want to accomplish.*

What *did* I want to accomplish while I played professional football—besides pay the bills? My research showed that the average "life expectancy" of a pro football player was four and a half years. How much could I do within that time frame? What could I do that I'd never done before? My list turned out to be short and simple:

1. I want to be on a Super Bowl team.
2. I want to lead the league in receiving.
3. I want to play and not get seriously injured.
4. I want to play at least five years and get my retirement.

Achieving these goals, however, did not appear to be easy. As soon as they were written on paper, my mind began to mock me: *You can't do it, Hinton. You're aiming too high! What makes you think you can ever get to a Super Bowl? Who do you think you are, wanting to lead the league! You'll never last five years! You can't play and not get hurt. Injuries are part of the game. The spine is delicate. Even wide receivers get surprise hits that could snap the old spinal cord and pucker your limbs.*

Having a family to provide for increased the fear of injury, and it began to haunt me constantly. This subtle twang of fear became a Chinese torture test before each game and at every practice. *Is this it? Will this be the one?* The few times I had been injured taught me that I couldn't play full out and be careful at the same time. So I lied to myself about the probabilities and the pain and played anyway. I just prayed to God for protection—both for me and my fellow players.

———◆———

My hankering for the best in life got the best of me. I could now afford to buy a house, and it had to be in Guilford, an exclusive suburb of Baltimore. Marcia shopped for houses while I practiced everyday. We enrolled Bart in a private school and immediately moved into the house she had located. There had been no reports of other blacks in the subdivision, but Marcia and Bart didn't seem to notice or care.

For the first few months, we shared our lives with the painters, the decorators, and the landscapers. Naturally, we had to have all new furniture and it made me feel extremely proud to be able to buy it for Marcia and Bart.

None of the neighbors baked cookies and brought them over, so Marcia, Bart, and I made up our own forms of family entertainment. There were several movie theaters nearby, and we all loved going to the zoo.

Nine-year-old Bart had devised a game to play during our frequent outings. He would pretend to be lost and would innocently ask a nearby victim, "Have you seen my Dad?" Of course the unsuspecting person would start to look around for this poor white kid's father, and then Bart would suddenly cry, "Oh, there he is—over there!" and point to me. He was an ornery little dickens, but I loved his sense of humor and his courageous determination to be himself. Marcia always told me he had "a very old soul," and if that meant he had wisdom beyond his years, she was correct. We jokingly called him "The Sage" whenever he demonstrated his incredible insight.

Bart and I loved each other very much and I carefully avoided trying to take the place of his biological father. Everytime I looked at his cherubic sleeping face though, I ached with the longing to be a good "Dad" to him.

Marcia and Bart took advantage of a pretty good mood one day when they asked me to go to the pet store with them. I never did like pets at all—especially in my house or in my car! That was a no-no to me. I wasn't too excited about strolling among the cages of yapping, barking dogs, until we came upon this Saint Bernard puppy. There he was, this little cuddly thing about two months old—big ears, big head, and big feet. I made the mistake of looking in his eyes . . . and the next thing I knew, we were walking out with him and two shopping bags full of doggie bargains! We decided to name him Bubba in honor of Bubba Smith, the Goliath-sized defensive end for the Colts.

Of course, I made Marcia and Bart *swear* that they would take care of Bubba. I ranted and raved . . . "I don't want that dog crappin' in the house! I don't want no dog hair in my car and I ain't feedin' him!"

Well, after about two weeks, Bart broke his arm, which meant *he* couldn't feed the dog. Then the next week, Marcia got sick, which meant *she* couldn't feed the dog. *I* wasn't going to feed him either, so I put ads in the paper to sell Bubba, trying to get my money out of him. Everyday, I'd come home and Marcia would say, "Well, some people called today, but they said we wanted too much money for him." Or, "They said they'd come by and look at him, but they didn't show up." Desperation set in. I knew I wasn't going to give the dog away because I had spent too much for him. The only thing for me to do was send him to obedience training. He was already getting too big to handle.

Bubba's first ride in my Lincoln was a trip to boarding school in the country. Every dog should be so lucky! He was sitting in the backseat, and I unconsciously repeated the mistake that had put me in this predicament. Looking in the rearview mirror, I saw two pitiful brown eyes staring questions of betrayal at me. It was almost like Bubba was crying out, "Are you takin' me away and leavin' me? How come you're doin' this to me—I ain't never done nothin' to you!"

I could hardly see through my own tears, but I kept driving. When I couldn't stand it anymore, I reached back, patted him gently, and assured him that I was only taking him to be trained. I promised him I'd be back soon.

After Bubba's graduation, "we" enrolled in a Saint Bernard club. The other members convinced me he was show material, so we entered competition for his breed. We won our share of ribbons; and anyway, who cared if he slobbered a little on the living room coffee table!

If Marcia and I weren't at dog shows or the zoo or the movies, we were home playing house. The four of us rambled around the 3,500 square foot structure and I was elated every time I came home to its beauty. Not only was it beautiful; it was spacious and bright and comfortable. Marcia was very talented with colors, form, and design; and the designers earned their money under her scrutiny. We ate in the formal dining room every night and even had candles on the table. This was a big deal for an Oklahoma kid who thought candles were kept on hand only in case of storms.

Bart shared the massive oak pool table with me. He used it to shoot nine ball, and I used it for tension therapy. The day before a game, I would crawl underneath the huge slab, stretch out on the cushy champagne carpet, and listen to Rod McKuen tapes for hours. At first, Marcia and Bart thought I was really weird, but before long they joined me in my sanctuary. They seemed to understand that my fear was unspeakable.

After the neighbors got over the shock of the Hintons homesteading in their territory, we eventually started receiving invitations to neighborhood parties and community functions. By the end of our first year in Guilford, we were THE couple to have. I was the only football player on the block and I could also dance. Marcia was friendly, beautiful, and intelligent. What more could a hostess want?

———◆———

Life in the locker room was similar to my early life in the Baltimore suburbs. I wasn't what you'd call the most popular player. I stayed to myself pretty much and didn't seem to fit the publicized patterns of a jock. When practice was over and I was through working, I wanted to be with my family and my dog.

The team joker was a black guy, 6′8″, and weighed about 250 pounds. Every time he passed my locker, he made singsong remarks like, "Oreo cookie—black on the outside; white on the inside. Oh, oh! Oreo!" I tried not to let his jibes get to me. He didn't know what was in my heart, so I decided to let it ride.

One day after a hard practice, he walked past my locker and recited his Oreo routine. My patience snapped. I'd had enough of his taunts. It was time to fight or flee. After slamming my locker door as hard as I could, I turned to face the source of my annoyance.

"Let me explain something to you, big guy," I began quietly. "You do not know anything about me, so let me give you some valuable advice." He backed up against his locker as I inched slowly towards him. "I'm the kind of guy who will leap into your heart *real* quick and keep you from breathing the rest of your life, so you better be careful," I warned. "Don't mess with me!"

I think the Oreo singer received my message. He hardly spoke to me after that.

And then there was the white guy who loved to make smart remarks about the way I dressed. He passed my locker one day and I could smell another confrontation in the air. "Hey, rookie! You shouldn't be spending all your money on clothes!" he jeered mockingly as he fingered the fabric of my silk shirt.

Now, all through college I was known as "Mr. Threads" because my wardrobe was stylish, colorful, and coordinated. Not only had he insulted my tastes, he had unknowingly insulted my title.

I stopped buttoning my shirt, stepped towards him, and looked him square in the face.

"Let me explain somethin' to you," I replied with icicles dripping from my words. "I believe in changin' clothes every day. I enjoy wearin' nice things, such as this silk shirt you just touched," I reminded him threateningly. "I've always had money and clothes and cars. Now, if that makes you unhappy, that's your problem," I said, pointing to his bare chest. "Why don't you just tend to your own business and let me handle mine!" I snapped.

"Well, uh . . . sure Eddie. I was just jivin' ya a little bit . . . no need to get upset," he backpedaled.

"I'm not upset . . . you'd know if I was upset," I added, flicking an imaginary piece of lint from my sleeve. "Now, if you'll excuse me," I said curtly, "I'll finish gettin' dressed."

Evidently the word got around that Hinton's temper shouldn't be tampered with, because there were no further incidents in the locker room.

My bark was worse than my bite, as the old saying goes. I knew I'd do anything to avoid a fight, but I hoped nobody would discover my lack of taste for violence.

13

THUMBS UP OR DOWN?

At last, my chance to be a starting player for the Colts arrived. I had been a benchwarmer for 6 pre-season and 11 regular season games. Now we only had three games left on the schedule, so the opportunities to prove myself were waning. Jimmy Orr and Ray Perkins, the two veteran receivers for the Colts, were out with injuries. The coaches gave me 24 hours' notice that I'd be the starting receiver against Dick LeBeau in the Detroit Lions game. I headed for the pool table.

It was raining the next morning when I left for the game, and wouldn't you know, it turned to sleet and snow just before kickoff time. The weather was a perfect match for the blast of cold fear that howled inside my heart.

The coach must have sensed my uneasiness. "Don't worry about making a mistake," he said as he sent me into the action.

"I don't," I replied sincerely. "Mistakes are part of my life."

His glance told me he wasn't sure if I was being a smart aleck or if I was serious. This was the moment I had been waiting for and I was determined to make it count. I would not be worrying about making mistakes.

Jimmy and Ray gave me advice on how to work against LeBeau and what to expect from him. LeBeau was known as one of the wiliest cornerbacks in the league and I was about to make my Colts debut against him. They told me he might try to push me around, but I was too eager to get discouraged by their warnings. I had watched LeBeau's techniques at every opportunity. He could not have studied my style, even if he had wanted to, because I had not seen that much action. My "rookieship" was definitely in my favor. The weather, however, was not.

The frigid turf was a nightmare for me as I knew it was for our quarterback, Earl Morrall. My first bungle occurred when I dropped one of Earl's perfect throws in the open. During the second quarter, I slipped while trying to make my cut, and LeBeau made the only interception of the game and scored on me. I switched to mud cleats while the scoreboard registered Lions 14; Colts 10. What was it the coach had said about making mistakes?

The Lion defense was extremely tough on Morrall and he was having to rush his passes. I had to set LeBeau up for my outside curl pattern by making inside moves on him, even on running plays. It finally paid off in the fourth quarter when Morrall plopped a 32-yarder into my almost-frozen paws and I entered the end zone for my first pro touchdown! The die-hard fans, bless them, unsnuggled from their stadium blankets long enough to applaud and cheer jubilantly. My frozen face felt like it would crack into shards as I slipped, slid, and smiled my way back to the sidelines. The extra point put us back on top, 17–14.

I read in the Baltimore newspapers the next day that my touchdown had stimulated our defense to hold Detroit at the 3-yard line. The Lions had eight chances to score, but with the clock running out, they had to settle for a field goal. The final score was 17–17, which seemed like a waste of everyone's energy, but I ended the game as lead-ing pass receiver with five catches, 134 yards, and six points. My rookieship had ended.

———◆———

A certain black ball player who sang Oreo songs, and a certain white guy who thought he was a wardrobe consultant, came up to me after the game and said, "Great game, Hinton! Looks like you're one of us now!"

I just shook my head and grinned, "No, I'm not one of y'all. I'm just the same Eddie Hinton who's been here all along."

———◆———

My second season with the Colts was almost a replay of my second season at O.U. Once again, I was blessed with new coaches. Don McCafferty replaced Don Shula as head coach for the Colts. Shula left Baltimore after the '69 season's eight wins, five losses, one tie, and a Super Bowl loss to the Jets. McCafferty waited eleven years to move up from his assistant coach position to the Colts' head man. I figured he was an expert by now, so when I read the Baltimore newspaper article quoting his opinion of me, I was elated:

"We intend to reward the people we feel play the best, even in pre-season. I want to see which players respond most to competition on the highest level . . . it makes our eyes pop to see Hinton out there. He flies . . . we thought Perkins and Hinton played well enough in Saturday's exhibition game against Oakland to warrant starting them both against Kansas City."

At last, I could get in the game.

———◆———

When the Kansas City Chiefs got to Baltimore, I was ready for them. I'd done my homework under Jimmy Orr's tutelage. He helped me unselfishly even though we were competing for the same position as starting receiver for the Colts.

The Kansas City game was fantastic for me, but as a team, we didn't fare so well. The Chiefs beat us, 44–24. My stats increased by 11 passes, 190 yards, and one touchdown. I had three opportunities to score, however, so I consoled myself with the adage, "There's always room for improvement." The Colt record for catches in a single game was set by Raymond Berry in 1957 when he grabbed 12 passes for 224 yards. This one game boosted me close to the top of the team's pass-receiving statistics. The chances were looking good that I would achieve at least one of the items on my personal goal list.

———◆———

The Colts had a winning streak for the next seven games—six divisional and one inter-conference. The AFL/NFL merger of 1966 was finally being implemented after much confusion over "who plays who" in the newly established conferences.

Ironically, our second loss of the season occurred in Miami, which was former coach Don Shula's new home. We called it the Dolphin Tank after Miami held us under and counted to 34 while we tried unsuccessfully to buoy our meager 17 points.

After winning two more inter-conference games against Chicago and Philadelphia, we journeyed to War Memorial Stadium and marched over Buffalo, 20–14 to cinch the AFC Eastern Division title. The tension and excitement mounted daily. Just a few more games to go and either the season would be over for the Colts or we would be one of the teams playing in the Super Bowl.

————◆————

McCafferty must have been trying to prove something, too. Under his excellent coaching direction, we won or tied all but two games in 1970's regular season play. After our victory over the Jets, it was a matter of "wait and see." Who would be our opponent in the AFC-Eastern Divisional playoffs?

The day after Christmas, quarterback Johnny Unitas led the Colts' stampede against the Cincinnati Bengals. The Baltimore defense held Cincinnati to 63 yards rushing and 76 passing for a 17–0 shutout. The very next game would determine whether I'd be attending the Super Bowl as a spectator or participating as a gladiator.

————◆————

The American Football Conference Championship game would afford me the privilege of playing against legendary Willie Brown of the Oakland Raiders. I had missed the opportunity earlier in the Colts' pre-season opener with Oakland. By the time I got to play in that game, Willie had already departed for the night. Without thinking of the possible consequences, I shot off my mouth to the coaches that I could beat Willie. The stakes had increased considerably since then. If we won this game, we would be on our way to Miami for Super Bowl V. It was time to put up or shut up.

For five months I'd been thinking about Willie. He was considered the number one bump-and-run cornerback in the league. Since I was trying to be the number one receiver, Willie presented my biggest challenge. Mentally, I was prepared for our confrontation and I felt like I could keep up with him all day long.

Unitas certainly gave me additional encouragement! During the game, he threw twelve passes my way. Although I only caught five of them, we managed to add 115 yards—almost half—to his 245 total yards passing for the game. At least we kept Willie busy!

Colt rookie Norm Bulaich also left his hoofprints on the Raiders with two touchdowns, and Ray Perkins scored a 68-yarder in the fourth quarter. Before a sellout crowd of 56,368 spectators, Baltimore captured its first AFC Championship title and earned the right to play in Super Bowl V against the Dallas Cowboys at the Orange Bowl. Having lost Super Bowl III to the Jets two years earlier, the Colts team was fanatically determined to lasso the Cowboys and tie them to the goal post.

14

SUPER BOWL V—BEST OR WORST?

"Take two weeks off and get prepared to play the greatest game in your life!" the coach had told us. Instead, I started playing mind games with myself, and I knew everyone of my teammates was doing the same thing. How much more could I do in two weeks that I hadn't been doing in the previous 14 weekly ballgames? What did he mean, "get prepared"? The conversation going on inside my head went something like this:

"You must be the best wide receiver in the league 'cause only the greats get to play in the Super Bowl!"

"No, you can't think that way, because you'll lose contact with reality . . . you're lucky to be here. You should maybe work on runnin' your patterns a better way. . . ."

"Well, why should I change? Maybe I better keep doin' the same thing I've been doin'."

"No, maybe you need to improve a little bit."

The phone rang constantly. Media people called for interviews. Their favorite question was, "Do you think you're going to win?"

I wanted to scream at them, **"Well, what do you think I've been workin' for all my life?!"**

The publishers called. "We're willing to give you ten thousand dollars to tell your story of the Super Bowl, because we feel like you're going to be an important figure in the game."

My mind said, "No, no, no! You can't think about that! Your attention has to be on football—it's gotta be on this game!"

Then the advertisers called. "Eddie, if you wear our shoes in the Super Bowl, we'll give you $5,000." I'd think, "My God, I could use $5,000 but it's not a good idea to switch now! Not for the greatest game in my life!"

By the time the first week of "vacation" had passed, I was about to go crazy and there was still a week to go! The tension and pressure mounted every day, which meant I spent a lot of time under the slab! Marcia and Bart hovered in my shadow and tried to keep the intrusions to a minimum. They did a fantastic job in spite of the fact that they were the brunt of my anxiety. Marcia was experiencing her own fears about the game. She had to journey to Miami with the other wives since the team would be sequestered in the hotel. Daily practices were already scheduled in Miami for the final week of "vacation," so I left her with the responsibility of making her own way to the Super Bowl.

———◆———

By the time January 17 rolled around, I was at such an emotional pitch that when I walked out onto the field in front of those 79,204 rabid fans, I felt like I was moving in slow motion. There were reporters, photographers, and television cameras everywhere. The noise from the stands did not penetrate my helmet, but the lights and colors and excitement surged through my body like mega-watts of electricity.

Two weeks off to *think*. Now it was time to react.

After interminable ado and ceremonial extravaganza, Super Bowl V opened its own chapter in the history books of professional football. The first quarter ticked off the clock as the two top teams in the nation got to know one another. Then it was my turn.

On the third play of the second quarter, in front of a sellout crowd and with an estimated 60-million TV viewers watching, Unitas threw the ball to me. It was a little high, and zipped across my fingertips. The next thing I knew, our tight end, John Mackey, had the ball in an armpit squeeze and was running toward the end zone!

I don't remember havin' this play in the practice sessions! I thought incredulously.

Mackey ran untouched to the end zone to complete the 75-yard touchdown play, and all hell broke loose.

The officials ran over to me, all of them shouting at once. ". . . touch it? . . . touch it?" was all I could hear through my helmet. I thought they were saying "Did you touch it?" so I nodded affirmatively and yelled "YEAH!" back at them while the crowd continued its nearly riotous complaints.

The referees called an official time out while they tried to confirm whether Mel Renfro, defensive back for Dallas, had touched the ball. The rules at that time were, if he *hadn't* touched the ball, it was an illegal play. The play was highly controversial, but they gave Mackey his six points for our side. Later in the game films, it was obvious Renfro tipped the ball, but at the time, that controversy set the tone for the rest of the game—utter bedlam.

Both defensive teams were at their best. There were turnovers, fumbles, interceptions, penalties, and injuries galore. The ball kept changing hands—back and forth, back and forth. "Are we ever gonna score?" I wondered, plaguing myself with deadly doubt.

Earl Morrall called a flea-flicker play that was supposed to work in the following organized manner: Morrall calls the snap. Hinton, as decoy, runs downfield to confuse the defense. Morrall pitches the ball to running back, Sam Havrilak. Hinton, undetected, runs to the end zone flag. Havrilak runs to the other side of the field and laterals the ball back to Morrall. Morrall throws the ball to Hinton and Hinton scores. But it didn't happen that way.

Earl got thoroughly sacked, leaving Havrilak with the ball. Havrilak, keeping his cool, threw the ball in my direction. I thought he was throwing it to me, but he was throwing to our tight end, John Mackey, who was standing behind me. Anyway, I caught the ball, turned upfield and was wide open! No one was in front of me and I was only ten yards from scoring.

What flashed through my mind as I ran was the trip to the Bahamas Marcia and I were going to take after I scored this touchdown and won this game! My mind strobed to the people in Oklahoma who were watching me about to score; then to all the wide receivers who wished they could have been where I was, but weren't. I was going to be great!

When I hit the five-yard line, Dallas' Cornell Green grabbed my elbow and the ball fell out of my hand! One ton of football flesh tried to wrap itself around a 14-ounce prolate spheroid that wouldn't stop bouncing. It was the most helpless feeling in the world as I belly-crawled the turf in pursuit of the pigskin that represented my $15,000 prize. I had blown it! I had just flushed an easy six points, a big fat check, *and* my greatness down the toilet in this "greatest game of my life."

The hardest person to face when I got back to the sideline was "Mad Dog" Mike Curtis, our linebacker. His nickname alone was enough to petrify most people, including me. The fact that we lockered next to each other would have no bearing on his possible reaction to my failure. Nobody said a word to me though, which only confirmed how badly I'd screwed up. This was the big time. There was no room or sympathy or language for mistakes.

The game grueled on as the teams smashed at each other unmercifully. With 7:35 left in the game, the score was tied, 13–13. I thought it would never end!

The Cowboys had their reins around our necks, but with 1:09 remaining, "Mad Dog" Mike intercepted a pass and put us on Dallas' 28-yard line. Two more plays left nine seconds on the Super Bowl clock and the score was still tied at 13. There had never been such a moment in my life, and I suspect there'll never be another to match it. The intensity literally crackled around the coaches, the players, the referees, and the fans.

When Jim O'Brien trotted out for the field goal, Dallas called a time out. Then they tried to call another one with no play in between, in hopes of rattling the kicker. Referee Schachter shook his head "no-no" while Morrall prepared for the snap and hold. When O'Brien expressed his concerns about the wind, Morrall assured him flatly, "There is no wind—just kick the ball straight." O'Brien's famous curveball kick veered through the goal posts for the Colts' first-ever Super Bowl win, 16–13.

————◆————

Dick Young of the New York Daily News summed up Super Bowl V when he wrote, "Have I just watched one of the greatest football games ever played, or the worst?"

I'm glad he didn't ask me.

My mind replayed it thousands of times, trying to change the reality of my disappointing performance. It haunted me all the way to the Bahamas, while an abandoned Super Bowl ring lay at the bottom of my duffel bag.

————◆————

Our trip to the Bahamas was a disaster. I could not shake my feelings of inadequacy, even though my team had won the Super Bowl. Rather than join in the frivolity and celebration that was taking place on sand-strewn beaches, I holed up in our hotel room or walked the grounds alone. I could not explain to Marcia what was going on inside me, since I didn't even know myself. For days, we argued or sulked, unable to communicate with each other.

Her experiences of the Super Bowl must have been a nightmare, too. She had been sick on the plane ride from Baltimore to Miami, and arrived at the Colts' bastion in misery. The other wives were met in the hotel lobby by their husbands, but Marcia's was annoyingly absent. I had not been in any mood to be around people prior to the big day, so the bellman had gladly escorted her to our room.

Marcia had sensed all along that the team management would have preferred a "no women allowed" trip. Naturally, they wanted all of our attention to be on the game, but they had to keep peace in the family. The wives would have rightfully squawked at any such exclusion, for they also had played an important part in the previous sixteen ballgames. Most of the women, including Marcia, were the stabilizing forces that kept the players' sanity intact.

On the morning of the Bowl day, the nervous women had been loaded on buses and transported to the stadium. Their player husbands had departed hours earlier in preparation for the game. Marcia arranged to sit with some of the other wives even though she didn't know any of them very well—we just didn't socialize with the team that much. She had told me what agony it was for her to watch the game, and laughingly admitted she had held her breath through most of it.

Elated at our win, the women had surged toward the field with thousands of raucous fans as their escorts. Marcia became separated from the group and felt frightened by her loss of direction. The players had been hustled into the locker room for endless congratulations and hours of interviews. Afraid that she might miss the bus to the hotel, or worse yet, the plane to Nassau, her feeling of panic had turned to despair. At last, she spotted some of the wives near the locker room ramp and politely shoved her way through the throng. When she stepped onto the field, a television camera, glaring lights and a microphone were thrust in her face.

". . . and here's one of the player's wives, now, I believe. How do you feel about your husband's win?" he demanded exuberantly, as she tried to keep the other ladies in sight. Unable to hear his question, Marcia just smiled into the lens and said proudly, "Hello, I'm Marcia Hinton, Eddie Hinton's wife!"

"Uhh . . . okay . . . well, uh . . . back to the locker room now folks!" he had stammered, smiling his plastic smile at the camera. Later, when Marcia was telling me all this, I tried to convince her that he had not meant to be rude. He had surely been instructed via his earphone to return the viewer to the locker room action. Marcia had just given me one of her "you don't understand" looks and burst into tears.

Jubilation was rampant on the plane ride to Nassau. Much to Marcia's humiliation, I slept most of the way, exhausted from the two-week "vacation" I had just taken.

Day after sunny day, we worked on our relationship in the privacy of our room instead of sipping tropical punch with our teammates by the pool. After four or five days of this "fun," it became unbearable for both of us. My depression and anger increased every time Marcia asked me to join in the activities. Finally, she packed her suitcases and announced her early and solitary return to Baltimore. Of course, this made matters even worse, so rather than try to talk her out of leaving, in which case I'd have to explain her absence, I crammed my things in my duffel bag and stalked after her. I left a hasty message at the hotel desk explaining an "emergency" that had just come up in Baltimore. We spoke to each other only out of necessity on the miserable plane ride home.

15

MISSION ACCOMPLISHED

From January to July of 1971, there was a constant repetition of celebrity activities for the Super Bowl winners. There were numerous invitations for me to speak at civic and community functions, most of which I gladly accepted. Charitable organizations asked me to help them raise money, and politicians sought me out in hopes of bolstering their campaign images.

I was also working during the off-season as a new car salesman for Monarch Lincoln/Mercury in Baltimore. Marcia and I had finally called a truce, and I was beginning to enjoy my notoriety. I also became an expert at avoiding all questions about my part in the Super Bowl.

I gave speech after speech at Baltimore schools, and always accepted opportunities to be with handicapped kids or those with learning disabilities. Before long, I was yearning for a child of my own, but I ran into a brick wall with Marcia on that issue. She already had a son, and was all too aware of the trials and tribulations that accompany the rearing of children. Marcia also knew of Bart's own particular problems because his mother's husband was black. She was unwilling to put this burden on an infant and there was no way to convince her otherwise. The cold war escalated.

When August finally arrived, I was anxious to get back to the turf. I had been inside the automobile showroom all summer long and was ready for some action and fresh air. Besides, there was something I needed to handle. As soon as play resumed, I would be on the lookout for ways to compensate for my haunting performance in the Super Bowl. As it turned out, I would just have to wait.

During the very first regular season game that year, I injured a groin muscle and for the next ten games, I tried to hatch that bench! Frustration and impatience were my companions on the sideline. Suiting up and sitting out were not my ideas of playing professional football.

My chance at absolution finally came on December 3, 1972, during the Colts' game against Buffalo. This was Johnny Unitas' final game in the presence of his hometown Baltimore fans. After 16 years with the Colts, he was on his way to the San Diego Chargers. He didn't play until late in the game, but when he made his appearance on the field, the crowd went absolutely wild. A plane circled over the packed stadium pulling a huge banner that read "UNITAS WE STAND."

When the cheering subsided enough for the audibles to be heard, he called a couple of plays that went nowhere. Then, on a third down, he dumped the ball over the head of one of the defenders, right into my up-stretched hands. I ran back 40 yards, eluded two charging Buffalo and scored six sacred points for the two of us. It was Johnny's last touchdown pass in front of his Baltimore fans; and it was my way of making up for the touchdown I should have scored in Super Bowl V.

The place went berserk. Fans tumbled out of their seats and streamed onto the field. People were screaming, crying, and hugging each other. Johnny was adoringly mobbed by the crowd and the game was delightfully delayed while the field attendants tried to restore order.

Johnny's memorable words to me on the sideline were simply and humbly, "Way to catch, Hinton!" The touchdown was no big deal to him, but by the gift of God, my path had been open to the end zone. The Cosmic Scorekeeper had given me a part to play in the drama of saying good-bye to one of America's premier quarterbacks. He left his worshipping fans with a touchdown pass and a win on the scoreboard. Johnny's down-home compliment also restored some of my self-esteem—just enough to face *my* inevitable future.

———◆———

Obsolescence occurs in football just as it does in any other business. As strategies shift and time moves on, so do the players, owners, coaches, and teams.

The handwriting was on the turf. The Colts were well-blessed with receivers, and the younger players were pressing for positions. They were strong and versatile; able to block *and* receive. They reminded me of someone I used to know.

I had played very little during the '72 season because of my injury, so I wasn't greatly surprised when, after four years with the Colts, I got put out to pasture.

———◆———

Marcia was stunned when I told her I had been cut. It seemed like we had just gotten "settled" in Guilford and were just beginning to adjust to our wonderful lifestyle. There was a red Porsche in the driveway, tennis lessons at the country club, and matching Rolex watches. Bart was doing super in school and Bubba was king of the block.

Yes, it probably meant we would be moving and no, I didn't know where.

I was just sort of numb. I knew it would happen sooner or later, so why did I feel so suddenly empty?

———◆———

The Houston Oilers picked up my contract for the '73 season and we sold the Guilford house to move south. We were trading the Atlantic for the Gulf and the suburbs for the city. The Oilers were just coming out of a one-win, thirteen-loss season, which didn't sound terribly exciting to me. (Much to my disgust, their one win had been over Baltimore.)

Marcia and I tried to place 3,500 square feet of household furniture into a 2,000 square foot apartment. It didn't work. We robbed Bubba of his backyard kingdom and plunked him down in a stamp-sized dog run. He wouldn't eat. Marcia went to work selling real estate and Bart was accepted in public school. They didn't like it. I stayed away from home as much as possible because I didn't like it either. I preferred to go practice with the losers who were trying to win; rather than stay at home with the winners who thought they had lost something.

I had never played on a losing team before, and since I needed a goal to tweak my interest, I decided to turn the Oilers around. Well, thirteen catches, 202 yards gained, and one touchdown did not turn the team around. I was surprisingly relieved when Houston cut me after one season. Meanwhile, back at the apartment, Marcia, Bart, and Bubba were expectedly apprehensive.

———◆———

The Boston Patriots needed a reinforcement for their battered corps of pass-catchers, so off I went to Massachusetts as a free agent to play for Chuck Fairbanks, the Pat's head coach. I'd played for him at the University of Oklahoma, and we knew each others' strengths and weaknesses. Two of the assistant coaches had formerly been with the Colts, so I felt like I was going backwards in time, rather than forward.

The other three members of my family stayed in Houston, where things were not going so well at home. Bart was suddenly a teenaged handful, and Marcia developed a case of chronic loneliness. Bubba was the only one who seemed to still like me, but I couldn't talk to him over the phone.

The future looked hopelessly dismal from where I was. By the end of the '74 season with the Patriots, I had enough years to get my retirement; I had ranked second in AFC pass receiving for a year; I had played on a winning Super Bowl team; I had my health, and I had played with some of the greatest football players of all time: Johnny Unitas, Earl Morrall, Mike Curtis, Bill Curry, Bubba Smith, Roy Hilton, and John Mackey—not to mention the heroic opponents we had faced together—Namath, Blanda, Bradshaw, Staubach and many others.

One evening after a strained long-distance phone call to Marcia and Bart, I pulled my yellowed, crumpled goal list from my wallet and slowly checked off the first three items. Led in receptions. Check. Won the Super Bowl. Check. Unimpaired. Check. My pencil stopped at number four, I said a silent prayer and drew a big black circle around it.

At the end of the season, I announced my retirement from pro ball.

16

ECHO FROM THE CHASM

You try not to believe you're different from everyone else in the world . . . until you're finished. Then it smacks you in the face. There is nothing to prepare the professional athlete for the world "out there."

Suddenly, I realized there was no purpose for me anymore and nothing to measure myself against. There were no games to win, no coaches to tell me what to do or how to do it, no huddles or pre-game meals, and no Tuesday morning film sessions to correct last week's mistakes.

Whenever a pro athlete wants to know how good or bad he is, all he has to do is look at his individual or team statistics, or pick up a newspaper, or listen to the applause, or look at the scoreboard, or deposit a paycheck.

Now there were no signs, rewards or status symbols, and without them, I questioned my worthiness. *Have I been fooling myself all along? Am I a loser after all?*

I had no idea what I wanted to do—what I could do. I had forgotten to plan for life *after* football. I worked for various companies in an effort to adjust myself to the world of business, but life continued on a downward spiral.

Marcia and I agreed to a trial separation that lasted about six months. We decided to give our marriage another chance; but after a few months of being together again, we both knew our relationship would no longer work. We had begun to replace all the good memories with bad ones, thereby invalidating the beauty of the past. Neither of us wanted that to happen, so we filed for divorce and part of me died.

Everything of meaning disappeared from my life. After eight years of marriage, my lovely wife and son were gone. My home was gone. My name in the newspaper was gone. My image as football hero was gone. My vision for Eddie Hinton was gone. My picture-tube life had gone blank and there wasn't even a courteous "technical difficulty, please stand by." I was dead in place.

Looking for aliveness, I spent night after night in Houston bars and even developed a daily routine to support the activity. I took naps in the late afternoon so I'd be ready to boogie as soon as the sun went down and the music came up. Every night of the week, I circulated in the darkness of forced frivolity. I tried anything that promised some relief from the emptiness: women, alcohol, pot, pills, cocaine—you name it, I tried it.

My experiments in deadening the pain of living provided only temporary relief. Every "morning after," I hated myself for the permanent damage I was inflicting on my body. After all, it had brought me a long way from Lawton, and hopefully, it had a long way to go.

My divorce from Marcia was final in 1977 and from then on, it was just me and good old Bubba. I had a Super Bowl ring in my drawer and a few bucks in my pocket, but there was nothing to take the place of the applause.

PART TWO

. . . and that tomorrow is a fantasy in our minds which never turns out how we fantasize it, whether good or bad. . . .

17

THE DUST BOWL GAME

It was my 29th birthday, and I had a bad case of the "lonelies." The only person I knew who possibly still loved me was Big Girl. I decided to go see her and to rationalize my trip, I told myself I would check around Lawton for some kind of business to get into. When a picture of me and Big Girl working together popped into my mind, a silent alarm sounded somewhere in my being.

Big Girl had changed the name of our house from "Geraldine's Place" to "The Dirty Thirty." The Dirty Thirties was an era of dust in the Great Plains States. Billowing clouds of misplaced topsoil had choked the inhabitants of the prairies and blanketed the parched land with total darkness even at midday. I could identify with these historical phenomena. That was me—Eddie Gerald Hinton—dark, desolate, and arid.

Almost two years had passed since my retirement from professional sports. I had sold cars and insurance, neither of which appealed to me as a life-long career. Was there anything "out there" that had my name on it? So far, my seemingly endless search for meaning had only led me to the bottom of a deep, dark, slippery, dangerous chasm. I just wasn't coherent enough to realize it.

———◆———

I could hear the music blaring as I drove in the driveway. When I walked in, Big Girl and a couple of her cronies were perched at the counter on bar stools, exchanging gossip, giggles, and slugs of beer. Big Girl recovered quickly from her surprise and gave me a warm welcome-home hug while the other ladies cooed their greetings.

There was a lone customer parked in front of the living room TV—a burly black man with drink in hand. He looked pretty far gone to me, so I didn't even say hello.

I continued to exchange pleasantries with the women and tried to explain to Big Girl why I hadn't called. It didn't matter, she decided—she was just glad to see me. She offered my autograph to her friends and they made a big to-do over finding some decent paper and a pen that would write.

"Eddie Gerald, why don't you buy me a drink!" the man slurred belligerently from the living room.

I continued to ignore him and began to sign my name for the women. "EDDIE HINTON . . . YOU HEAR ME? BUY ME A DRINK!" he hollered, as my hackles sprang into readiness. The women stopped their chittering and glanced at each other nervously.

He swayed in his chair and peered at me glassy-eyed, waiting for me to join him at his table. Well, his invitation deserved an R.S.V.P., all right. I'd seen plenty of his type—killing someone meant nothing to them. If you didn't respond to their distorted reality, they took it as a definite sign of weakness, and would come at you.

My experience in special education taught me to always reach the level of the student. I knew there was no way to psyche this guy—he wouldn't understand nice talk. I started towards him, my eyes registering his every blink. I could yell awfully loud—it's one of the things I got an "A" for in practice—so I turned up the volume with each step.

#1

#2

Grandmother Odessa, my
first on-the-job supervisor

My father, Eddie L. Hinton

#3

My mother, Geraldine Hinton,
before she became "Big Girl"

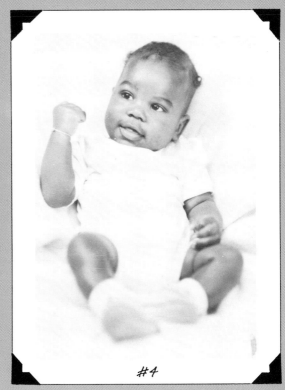

I had
something
to say, even
at three
months old!

#4

#5

Me, Mama and Walter with our newest toys

Me and the
jukebox,
waiting to be
fed.

#6

#7

I wanted a horse — they gave me a football

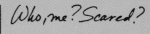
Who, me? Scared?

#8

#9

Portrait of an athlete

#10

Practicing the hurdles, and getting ready for life

#11

Big Red Sooners — here ↓ come!

Doing
everything
the hard
way —
broken
handed
receiver

#12

#13

I know what to do — just give me the ball

#14

Running with a football under one arm and fear under the other.

ELKHART MOTOR HOTEL
ELKHART, INDIANA

Indiana's finest motor hotel with completely new fa-
cilities for groups, businessmen and families. Only 2
miles from the Toll Road in downtown Elkhart—center
of the shopping and theater district. Completely air
conditioned. Free overnight parking. Dine in famous
Redwood Room and 24-hour Coffee Shop. 200 beautifully furnished rooms. Reservations: Phone (219)
JA 4-1800.

POST CARD

Address

Mother,
    I am getting ready
For the game, Going
Out to do my best
        your Son,
        Eddie Gerald

#572

Mrs. Geraldine Hinton
1325 Washington St.
Lawton, Oklahoma
                73502

#15

An early major commitment

#16

Sooner or later, I made it

#17

Heading for my
next goal...

#18

#19

Six-year weekend soldier

#20

Marcia Hinton,
my lovely wife
for eight years

#21

Barton Pace, the 7-year-old sage

#22

Me and Baby Bubba

#23

First, you catch the ball...

#24

...then, you score! AFC Championship Game

XD BRA034 MG PDF CHICKASHA OKLA SEP 29 1970 1040A CDT

EDDIE G HINTON

  311 SOUTHWAY BALTO

WOW - YOU WERE MAGNIFICENT, SENSATIONAL. OKLAHOMA SPORTS

CASTERS AGREE. OUR VERY BEST

  AUDREY AND LELAND

        417P EDT.

#25

A telegram from Marcia's parents meant
more than the game stats.

My short-term
modeling career

#26

#27

Mmmm, cream cheese brownies

Y'all have
helped me so
much in my
business

#28

#29

Cash Taylor, my miracle horse

#30

Polo action in the game of kings

#31

Cutting is an excercise in concentration.
Roping ... well, I'm working on it !

#32

Big Fella blessed me with strong, versatile hands

"DO YOU REALIZE WHAT I'VE DONE FOR YOU? I'VE PUT THIS PLACE ON THE MAP! I'VE GONE AND PLAYED FOOTBALL AND I'VE BEEN ON TV AND PEOPLE ALL OVER THE WORLD KNOW WHO I AM AND THAT I'M FROM LAWTON, OKLAHOMA AND YOU ASKED *ME* TO BUY *YOU* A DRINK?!? YOU SHOULD BE BUYIN' ME SUMTHIN'! Y'ALL SHOULD HAVE A BAND OUT THERE WAITIN' ON ME! YOU SHOULD PRAISE ME WHEN YOU SEE ME . . . BUT WHAT DO Y'ALL DO? . . . YOU ASK *ME* TO BUY *YOU* A DRINK! YOU ARE PATHETIC!"

By this time, I was about six inches from the end of his nose and he had sobered up considerably during my short walk. Big Girl appeared between us like a pro referee and steadied him on his way to the door.

———◆———

On Sunday, I headed back to Houston, but my thoughts remained in Lawton. The night before, Big Girl had called her friends and neighbors to come over because "Eddie Gerald's home." My objections were overruled by her insistent, "But it's your birthday!" So instead of visiting with my mother, I spent the evening avoiding repetitive questions from tipsy strangers about the Super Bowl win.

Big Girl had given me a little plaque for my birthday. It was quite out of character for her—she usually gave me a bottle of shaving lotion. The inscription on the plaque read, "Just trust yourself, then you will know how to live." I didn't know what Mr. Goethe meant, but his words had a certain ring to them and kept nibbling at my brain.

I thought about the drunk who had escaped my wrath the previous afternoon, and I felt a mixture of pity and loathing for him. Suddenly, *his* face became *my* face and I broke out in a cold sweat. *That could have been me,* I thought, agony filling my chest. "That *will* be me, if I don't change my ways," I blurted out loud in the car. The mental picture was so devastating, my hands began to shake on the steering wheel. I had to pull off the highway and stop. I couldn't see where the road was. The tears washed over my eyelids and I hugged the steering wheel for dear life.

When I finally got home to my empty apartment, I was accompanied by the same question I had been trying to answer since childhood. *What can I do to be good?* Now I knew the answer would not come from the past; nor would it come from the placebos I flushed down the commode.

Living in the question was pure torture.

18

MONEY MANAGEMENT 201

After my birthday trip to Lawton, life took on new meaning for me. I was suddenly obsessed with the desire to make something out of the rest of my life. The waste and despair I had seen in the mirror of the drunk's face kept me "straight." I stopped hanging out in bars and began to read about business. The artificial relief that I had found in bottles and plastic bags was replaced with a determination to once again succeed at something—*anything*. I set new goals in my job as an insurance salesman, and began to realize how much I really cared for people.

All the while, I kept looking for that "something bigger than football" to fill my life. Whenever my spirits were low, I'd dig in my dresser drawer for the quarantined Super Bowl ring. Just holding it in my hand seemed to give me renewed energy, strength, and courage. Surely if I had been good enough to earn such a coveted prize, then I could use those same qualities to build my future. I thought of the physical, mental, and emotional demands I had placed upon myself in order to receive this token of distinction. Then one day, I admitted the truth. There was nothing that would ever match that level of agony and ecstasy again. But I knew I was ready and willing to find the next best thing.

What really appealed to me was the thought of being able to tell people, particularly athletes, about my experience of professional sports and the chasm from which I had just emerged. Maybe they wouldn't have to make some of the mistakes I had made. When I casually discussed this with friends, their consensus was that first I'd have to have some kind of credibility if I wanted people to listen to me. How could I "hang a shingle" without some kind of track record in the "real" world? Their conclusion was that I needed a successful business. This rationale made sense to me, so I started looking for a business to get into.

But first things first. I knew I didn't even have the basics, the fundamentals of business. All I knew was athletics, special education, and sales. I enrolled in every free seminar and workshop I could find. It was amazing how many were available, once I started looking. I took classes on diction, writing composition, business law, bookkeeping, and how to start a small business.

If I was planning to give speeches one day, I would need to know how; so I joined the Toastmaster's Club to learn about public speaking. I even signed up with a modeling agency to reinforce my self-confidence. The agency sent me out for a few local commercials and I was thrilled to accept a bit part in a film. My friends thought this was a big deal, but after a few days on the set, I realized the world of film was much too slow for me. Standing around waiting for someone to say "action" was beyond my patience.

Much of my time was devoted to studying, and my insurance sales began to reflect my priorities. I needed income that was more dependable, because the cash flowing in didn't match the cash flowing out.

When I saw a help-wanted ad for a box salesman, it caught my eye. Container Corporation of America offered training seminars in conjunction with the position. I applied for and got the job. It felt pretty good to have an attache case, a company car, and an expense account. As long as I added my share to the bottom line of the company, my time was my own.

Selling seemed to be easy for me. Or at least, talking to people was easy for me; and in the process of our conversations, they usually bought something. There were cold calls, business lunches, sales reports, and staff meetings. Although I was busy, I wasn't very physically active. Most of my time was spent inside stale, fluorescent-bathed offices, and I was starting to gain weight from all those lunches. I kept telling myself: "No, no, no, Eddie! You'll end up like Big Girl!"

I guess you could say I was content, but I was not satisfied. I was making good money for the amount of work I was doing, but my lifestyle had not improved any.

I figured I needed to show some stability if I was ever going to be a businessman. The ones I knew about lived in nice houses, and I was still crammed into a rather dingy apartment.

One of my friends was in real estate, so I took her to lunch and outlined my plan. I wanted to buy a house with little or no money down, and I wanted the lowest possible monthly payments. She assured me the time was right to make such a purchase and recommended a new subdivision in southwest Houston. There were houses in all stages of construction, and I might be lucky enough to find one near completion.

The house I liked was perfect for me. It had a large master bedroom and bath, complete with shower and Jacuzzi. I had no idea how I was going to fill the other two bedrooms, nor did I know when I might have occasion to eat in the dining room. The living room had a fireplace, beamed ceilings, and a wall big enough to hold the massive bookcase I'd hauled from Baltimore to Houston another lifetime ago. I used it to display all my trophies and sports memorabilia, as well as a picture of Bubba. He would not get lost in our new yard, but it was better than a chain-link dog run.

I handed over $500 earnest money for the house and signed my name to the builder's contract. I had no idea where the rest of the money was going to come from, but I knew if God meant for me to have a house, He'd surely show me the way. Big Fella and I were on good terms again. He had lovingly accepted my apologies for being aloof so long.

The realtor told me I could borrow money through a mortgage company. I had no idea how these matters worked, because Marcia had handled the purchase of the Guilford house. My friend advised me to locate a mortgage company; and within it, find a young, aggressive guy about my age who was in a position to make a decision about my loan.

I was driving home from work one day and saw a mortgage company that was easy to get to from the freeway. I navigated the exit ramp, the intersection and the parking lot; said a prayer and strolled inside. The receptionist was slightly frumpy and looked at me rather strangely when I asked for a young, aggressive mortgage man. She went to the back of the suite and returned with a guy about my age, who was obviously much too short for his weight.

He invited me to follow him to his office, and on the way, we passed some very big offices with some very big executives sitting at their very big desks.

Somehow, I just knew this was my guy. I decided not to mention my pro career yet, for two reasons: My experience had taught me that most men are intimidated by athletes; and I was afraid he would ask me where all the money had gone. Of course, he'd eventually know everything about me, if I accomplished the purpose of my visit; but I planned to tell him later and pretend modesty about my achievements.

"I want to buy a house," I began forthrightly, after sitting down in the straight chair across from his laminated desk top.

"Well, great!" he smiled congenially. "That should be no problem! You've certainly come to the right place!" he assured me.

"Oh, yeah, there's gonna be some problems," I laughed, "but it's obvious to me that you're smart and capable," I added, looking at his brass name plate.

"Well, I do know my job pretty well," he admitted proudly. "Now, Mr. Hinton, tell me about the house you want to buy," he said, turning to a fresh sheet of yellow legal pad paper.

When I finished telling him all the details, I drew a sketch of the floor plan on his tablet. Then James adjusted the glasses on his nose and asked the crucial question:

"Well, Mr. Hinton, what's your salary?" he asked with pencil poised.

"I'll tell you right now James, it's probably not enough to buy this house; but I promise you, I can make the loan payments every month," I replied hastily, even though I had no idea what the amount might be.

He hesitated and rubbed his chins anxiously. "But you've gotta have twice or three times your salary to qualify for this house," he said uncomfortably.

"I understand what you're sayin', James," I sympathized, "but my whole life has been about meetin' challenges and goin' for it. I don't know much about the mortgage business, but I know what it takes to keep my word. I'm confident that where there's a will, there's a way," I concluded politely.

"Well," he said, "let's go ahead and fill out an application and see what happens. Maybe I can walk this one through the channels," he offered hopefully.

"Great, James! Whatever you say! You just let me know what information you'll need and I'll get it for you," I replied. "I'm used to goin' around obstacles," I laughed truthfully.

"So am I," James replied seriously. "But I haven't learned to leap tall buildings, yet," he mused as he wrote my name across the top of a manila file folder.

———◆———

On moving day, I called James to give him my new phone number.

"Hey, man, this house is great! I can stretch my arms in the bathroom and not get a ceramic knuckle sandwich and my dog's runnin' and playin' in the yard and I've already met my new neighbors and . . ." I slowed down to breathe, ". . . and I just wanna thank you for gettin' it all handled!"

"Well, you're welcome," he laughed at my exuberance. "Just remember us when the 15th rolls around!" he reminded.

"Don't you worry 'bout that," I assured him. "I done told you I can make the monthly payments and I promised I wouldn't let you down!"

There you go again, Hinton—shootin' off your mouth! When are you ever gonna learn?!

"Say, Eddie," James said in afterthought, "would it be too much trouble to ask if you could send me an autograph for my boy? He's playing in little league this year, and it sure would give him a thrill," he asked politely.

"Sure thing, James!" I answered, "I'll put one in the mail just as soon as I unpack and can find a stamp in all this mess!"

19

FIRST, YOU GET A BUCKET

The noose was beginning to tighten. I knew I had to find a business that would support my newly-acquired stability symbol. I was extremely proud of my sales commission checks from Container Corporation, but they just didn't stretch far enough. I began to think of all the money I'd invested in ridiculous tax shelters when I was playing pro ball, and I wished I had it now to pay for *my* shelter!

In pro football, whenever somebody got cut or couldn't play anymore, the inside locker room joke was:

"Whatever happened to old so-and-so?"

"Oh, he done gone to the car wash."

That voice in my head kept whispering, *Eddie Hinton done gone to the car wash!*

———◆———

I dialed Gregg Bingham's phone number. I had great respect for the position he had played with the Oilers when we were teammates during the '73 season. His job as middle linebacker was similar to the quarterback's, except on the other side of the scrimmage line. He directed the defense, which was as crucial to winning as calling the

111

plays. He owned and operated a chain of coin-operated car wash businesses in Houston.

"Hey, man! This is E.G.!" I greeted boisterously through the phone.

"Hey, how you been, home-boy?" Gregg replied warmly. "It's been awhile since I heard your voice! What you been up to lately?" he asked.

"Oh, I'm sellin' boxes and paper for Container Corporation . . . doin' all right, I guess," I replied dubiously. "Say, man, I need to talk to you! I got some questions I want to ask you about the car wash business," I said, getting right to the point.

"Well, you're talking to the right person," he laughed. "You interested in maybe buying a location?" he questioned, suddenly at attention.

"Well, no, I'm just askin' around . . . seein' what the other guys are up to. I need to find me a business of my own, you know what I mean? It takes too long to get anywhere, workin' for someone else," I said with frustration.

"I hear you, hom'. That's why I started my own company," he reflected. "The car wash business ain't bad, Eddie. You might be interested after you see some of the reports I've been keeping. Why don't we have lunch this week and you can take a look," he offered generously.

"Sounds good, hom'. You buyin'?" I laughed, remembering some previous lunch tabs. This guy could eat more than me!

"Hinton, you haven't changed a bit!" he laughed. "Yeah, I'll buy again," he added jokingly. "Better yet, why don't you meet me at my car wash behind Sharpstown, then we'll grab a bite to eat. How 'bout Thursday?"

"Let me look here," I said, checking my calendar. "That oughta work fine—I don't have anything scheduled."

The car wash concept was simple. Customers drove in under a building that looked like a carport; got out of their cars to put quarters in the slot; water and wax came out of flexible rubber hoses connected to the ceiling; and, if aimed accurately by the customer, a dirty car became a clean car after the personalized power-shower.

We continued our conversation over laden trays at Wyatt's Cafeteria. Gregg was enthusiastic about his business, and shared his knowledge openly.

"Eddie, all you need for a car wash is a good location. Find a good spot and I'll help you put it together," he urged, anxious to help a buddy.

"Well, I don't know, man . . . I'm kinda strapped right now . . . just moved into my new house and my capital is kinda depleted . . . I was just checkin' my sources and doin' some research . . .," I trailed off, discouraged at the situation I had put myself in.

Gregg ignored my hesitation.

"Well, just don't say no too quick, E.G.!" he admonished. "Drive around and see if you spot something. Look over those reports I gave you, then we'll get back together. Car wash ain't a joke to me, hom'," he concluded solemnly.

That night, I propped myself up in front of a cable television rerun and went over the figures Gregg had given me. The numbers were impressive, so I decided to scout for a "good" location on Saturday morning when traffic would be light.

I was driving Houston's streets by 7:00 am, eyes peeled for possible car wash sites. Around noontime, I was driving past Hobby Airport when a vision appeared in the sky. I didn't know it was a vision at the time, but it miraculously turned into one.

A small airplane zoomed overhead on its landing approach, and as I glanced up at it, a question popped into my head: *I wonder who washes airplanes?* My thoughts began to dance! *They ain't much bigger than a car or truck, and in the same amount of time it would take to wash a car, I could wash an airplane and maybe make three times the money!*

If I could come up with a way to put a water tank and some hoses on wheels, then I could wash airplanes at any airport in Houston! At least, my idea was worth investigating.

My fingers walked through all the sections in the yellow pages that had anything to do with aircraft and cleaning. There were no listings for a mobile aircraft cleaning service.

If I had a water tank on the back of a truck . . . and a machine I could turn on . . . the water goes through the machine . . . it gets mixed with soap . . . bubbles come out the other end . . . squirt it on the airplane . . . a bright shiny plane emerges. Simple! My dining room table was covered with sketches and crumpled notes.

For a week or more, I massaged the figures. If I washed seven airplanes a day at $45 a plane, regardless of the size . . . and if I got a hundred planes . . . and if I had ten trucks out there . . . I could make a million dollars in a year and my overhead would be like $350,000 . . . and what in the world would I do with that other $650,000? I was too inexperienced to know that writing it on paper was not the same as making it happen. I did that in football, but I forgot I was in the "real" world now.

I had never even driven a truck before, but I was already telling my friends, "I'm gonna go clean airplanes!" I also imagined washing trucks, sidewalks, parking garages, office buildings, houses, mobile homes, statues . . . I could clean anything!

Nobody had ever heard of the concept before, but, ironically, everyone had some advice:

"If you get a truck, get a Ford truck."

"Well, why a Ford instead of a Chevy or Dodge?"

"'Cause they're more durable."

"Oh, okay! Thanks!"

I started reading up on trucks.

———◆———

It was late in the day to be eating lunch, so the buffet selection was slightly limited. That was okay with me—I had been looking at trucks most of the morning and I didn't want to have to make any major decisions about what to eat.

Most of the sections in the restaurant were closed, so after loading my plate at the buffet, I sat down near another late eater, and began to tackle my meatloaf.

"Excuse me," the man said. "Aren't you Eddie Hinton? Played for the Oilers?" he asked with certainty.

"Uh, yessir . . . I am," I answered politely. I had a hunch my mashed potatoes were going to get cold.

"My name's Louis . . . Louis Thorpe," he stretched across the small tables and shook hands. "I've watched you play a lot. You played for Baltimore, too, didn't you?" he questioned, waiting for confirmation.

"Yessir, and Oklahoma, too," I added proudly.

"I'm an O.U. alum, too," Mr. Thorpe exclaimed. "What are you doing now that you're out of football?" he asked with a curious smile.

"Uh, . . . I'm sellin' paper for a paper company," I replied as I tipped the catsup bottle over my meatloaf and spanked it vigorously.

There was an awkward silence while I concentrated on my lunch. Then, something inside me said, *Hinton, why don't you ask him what he does for a living?*

"What do you do for a livin', Mr. Thorpe?" I asked. He looked rather surprised that I had resumed the conversation after such a long pause.

"I'm President of Port City Ford," he answered casually.

"FORD?" I shot back incredulously. "You sell Ford trucks?"

"Well, yeah," he replied nonchalantly.

I practically attacked him in my excitement. "You're the guy I need to talk to! I'm gettin' ready to buy ten trucks and we're goin' to wash airplanes and we're goin' to travel all over Houston," I said in one breath.

He looked a little confused and overwhelmed, so I backed off and started over. "I'm gonna start a mobile aircraft cleaning business. I need a truck so I can get out there and do the cleaning myself at first. After I learn everything I need to know, then I'm gonna expand my fleet and offer this service throughout Houston." I stopped to let the translation sink in.

"Hmmmm. That's interesting," he said, rubbing his chin.

I proceeded to tell him all the calculations I'd gone through and all the research I'd done.

"That's a new one on me, Eddie. I never heard of that kind of business," he confessed when I finished. "I've got to get to a meeting by 3:00, but why don't you come see me at my office," he suggested. He gave me his card; we shook hands again, and I assured him I would call.

Now I was scared. Maybe somebody believed me.

For two days I mulled over the possible meeting with Mr. Thorpe. Was I being too hasty? How far should I pursue my idea? Was I sure I wanted to start my own business? What if I couldn't make it? That old familiar voice of self-doubt pumped its poison through my mind and paralyzed any action I was contemplating.

As I unpacked the moving boxes that were still stacked in my living room, I came across the plaque Big Girl had given me for my birthday. The words that had had no significance suddenly found an ear in my heart. "Just trust yourself, then you will know how to live." I went straight to my tool box, got out the hammer and a nail and hung the plaque next to the refrigerator. Then I went directly to the phone and called Mr. Thorpe to set up our appointment.

After re-establishing our acquaintance, I explained again what I was trying to do. I hoped my nervousness appeared to be enthusiasm.

"Well, Eddie, do you know if you're going to use pressure or steam to clean the planes?" he asked, trying to determine my needs.

"Ummm . . ." I began uncertainly. "Well, I don't know. That's what I'm tryin' to find out right now," I admitted candidly.

"That will be pretty important to know, so we can decide what size trucks to order. Have you been out to the airport to see how the big guys clean those 727's?" he drilled. "I imagine whatever they do for a big one would work for a little one."

"No, sir, I haven't been out there yet, but I plan to go," I said, suddenly feeling the way I used to feel when I missed a homework assignment.

He called in his sales manager and said, "Why don't you take Eddie out to Intercontinental and y'all take a look at the place and see how they do it."

"I don't have any money to put this thing together," I interrupted politely. "Y'all may just be wastin' your time," I warned them graciously.

"Don't worry about it," Mr. Thorpe assured me. "Ford Motor Credit Company will finance it and give you a purchase order if you're going to put equipment on the trucks."

"They will?" I blurted out naively, then quickly recovered. "Well, uh . . . I could run out there tomorrow afternoon if that fits your schedule," I volunteered. These folks didn't waste time! They were serious, and I was suddenly panic stricken.

———◆———

We learned from our trip to Houston's largest airport that the big boys used pressure instead of steam. That meant I needed a generator and a pressure washer. More advice poured in from my friends.

"Eddie, if you're going to get a self-contained generator, get an Onan," one of them had told me authoritatively.

"What's an Onan?" I asked in genuine puzzlement.

"An Onan is the brand name of a generator that's used in motor homes."

So I ordered an Onan, and Mr. Thorpe and I put the truck deal together. I finally located a 300-gallon water tank, and my mobile cleaning unit was almost complete. All I had to do was have my company name painted on the truck and find some customers. Now that I was in business for myself, I said "hello" and "good-bye" to my final pay check from Container Corporation and gave them back their car. I had a truck of my own now.

The truck loomed like a giant water bug in my driveway. I'd stare out the window at it and then I'd go sit in it. I could hardly wait to get my Onan. Turn the machine on . . . water and soap comes out . . .

One day soon, I knew I'd have to go to the airport and wash something!

———◆———

There was a small airport in the southwest part of Houston. I called to get the owner's name and made an appointment to go see him.

I drove out to Hull Field, found Mr. Hull's office, and introduced myself. "Doc," as everyone respectfully called him, was a gruff, burly-chested, slow-talking entrepreneur. Hull Field was the first privately-owned business in Sugar Land, historical home of Imperial Sugar Company. He started his little airport in 1954 on $400 he borrowed to make the down payment on 250 acres of flat-as-a-pancake land. Then he borrowed a motor grader to build his first runway. His early effort had certainly paid off. I figured the airport was worth around $15–20 million. He should know something about small airplanes!

Mr. Hull leaned back in his swivel chair, formed a steeple with his fingertips and listened while I told him what I was trying to do. Then I made my humble plea.

"The reason I came to see you is I don't know how to wash an airplane, and I figured if anybody could teach me, you could," I stated succinctly. "Will you help me learn the language and show me what to do?" I asked, faking more courage than I felt.

He sat upright in his worn leather chair and looked me straight in the eyes. "I'll tell you what, Hinton. I have a wash rack right outside this office and I'm willing to tear that thing down if you're planning to learn to wash airplanes. When I'm out there on that ramp talking business to some prospective customer, and some fly-in is washing his plane, the spray and soap comes all the way over to where I'm standing and attacks me. It irks me to no end. Then the hose gets run over and snapped off the faucet and I have to buy a new one. If you're serious about this mobile unit, then I think I can work with you," he finished with a tiny hint of doubt as to my commitment.

"Well, Mr. Hull, I'm serious, all right. I've got a $21,000 truck, a generator, and a water tank sittin' out there in your parkin' lot, just waitin' to pay for itself," I replied forthrightly. "I'll appreciate any help you can give me," I said, resting my case.

We scheduled a time to get together for my first airplane washing class. On my way out, I made a mental note to take some of my homemade cream cheese brownies for recess. This new teacher deserved something far better than an apple!

20

THEN YOU BAKE BROWNIES

Washing airplanes was long, hard, greasy, monotonous work. It was comparable to playing football with at least twenty pounds of equipment on, whether the weather was hot or cold, wet or dry. My only consolation was the obvious uniqueness of my new business—there wasn't any other fool out there doing what I was doing!

Morning pep talks occurred daily in front of my bathroom mirror. I had to stay "pumped," and these self-directed cheers sent me into the day's business with purpose.

The monthly payment-due notice finally found its way to my new mailbox. My new bed in my new house was a place of wonderment. I wondered how I was going to make my new payments!

The dotted line had long since been signed for the truck and equipment, and I expected the payment coupons any day. As the old saying goes in football when a situation gets critical, it was "third and long."

The cleaning jobs trickled in slowly. Each day, the calendar reminded me of my obligations and the growing stack of bills was the proverbial string around my finger.

I was more than antsy about making my payments—I had given my word. I wished I had had some marketing courses at O.U. How could I let people know about my business? How could I let them know they needed me? What could I do to get some attention without adding to the "please remit" stack? I knew I had to find a way to get more business.

————◆————

A friend of mine was having a party and I had been invited. I didn't go to parties much anymore, so I turned down the invitation. At the last minute, something prompted me to change my mind, and I decided to go.

There was a woman at the party named Eloise who owned and operated her own restaurant. We got into a discussion about owning your own business and she invited me to eat at her cafe. She bragged about having the best chicken-fried steak in Houston, and the next day I went to check it out. It was one of the best I'd ever eaten.

While waiting for Eloise to bring my check, I was looking the place over and got a perfect idea for a major Eddie Hinton ad campaign. There was a chalkboard on an easel that listed "Daily Desserts." I wasn't interested in eating any, but it gave me an inspiration on how to promote myself.

On cold winter nights in Baltimore, Marcia and I had baked delectable cream cheese brownies. Wouldn't the newspapers print a story about an ex-pro athlete who baked brownies? Not just *brownies*, but *cream cheese brownies*! The thought instantly appealed to me, and I could already see the headline: "Macho Man Makes Millions On Munchies." My imagination was running wild!

Eloise's restaurant would be a good place to test-market the brownies, so when she brought my check, I approached her on the idea.

"Say, Eloise, where do you get them desserts you're talkin' about on the chalkboard?" I asked, waving my hand toward the easel.

"Well, the cakes and pies we order from the bakery . . . the custard we make right here in our own kitchen," she replied after some thought. "Why?" she asked hopefully, "you want to order something?"

It was time for me to jump in there and stir up my idea. "Nah, I'm full up. But I was just wonderin', do you suppose people would be interested in some brownies?" I sat forward in my chair and continued confidentially. "Now, I'm not talkin' about just any brownies, I'm talkin' about *cream cheese* brownies from a very famous recipe and they are deeeelicious!" I drawled, demonstrating my guarantee.

"Well . . . I don't know. My customers would probably try 'em, especially if they're homemade. Do you know somebody who makes 'em?" she asked, clearly interested at this point.

"Yeah!" I replied. "Me!"

"You?" She looked at me like I was crazy. "I thought you were in the airplane cleaning business!" she guffawed in surprise.

"I am, but my hobby is baking," I answered, stretching the truth a little, "and if I bake anything, I either have to eat it or give it away. Might as well sell 'em to you, if you're interested."

"Well, I guess we could try it once or twice and see what happens. How much would we charge?" she wondered aloud.

"Well, it depends on how big a piece you think you should serve. I can sell 'em to you by the pan, or I can put each square in plastic wrap and you can charge however much you want." Suddenly, my simple idea was turning into an all-out plan. The thought of wrapping hundreds of tiny squares didn't sound like much fun, but it was too late to retract my hasty words.

"Friday's my best day for desserts . . . people like to start celebratin' the weekend, you know," she laughed. "Why don't you bring me a pan on Friday and I'll write 'brownies' on the chalkboard."

"Okay! Great! I'll be in here Friday mornin'. What time do you open?" I quizzed.

"We open for breakfast at 6:00 am—do you think you could bring 'em by around 5:30? I'll be here then, for sure," she promised.

"Uh, 5:30? Well, sure! I'll beat the traffic that way," I said, grimacing inside. I began to wonder what I had gotten myself into. "By the way, Eloise, would you do me a favor? When you write that on the board up there, could you squeeze in *'Eddie Hinton's cream cheese'* brownies?"

———◆———

The tender, succulent squares were a success at Eloise's. After the second week of sales, I knew it was time for Eloise to call the newspapers and let them in on this unique story. I made sure she had my phone number in case they wanted to call for an interview.

Several days went by, and then a newspaper reporter called. In addition to wanting an interview, he wanted to take pictures of me removing a pan of freshly baked brownies from my new oven! The article appeared in the paper, giving information about my sports career, my new aircraft cleaning business, and my hobby of baking. The phone began to ring, much to my excitement, but instead of getting orders to wash airplanes, I got orders to bake brownies!

Before I knew it, I was baking three nights a week from 6:00 pm 'til 3:00 in the morning. I had to get up at 5:00

am and deliver the goodies, then go clean airplanes all day.

The schedule got too tough to manage, so I enlisted the help of some of my friends who thought it would be fun to bake and wrap brownies. Most of them helped once or twice, then never came back.

The brownie assembly line lasted about six months. I was making anywhere from $100–$300 a week on my "hobby" after expenses. This sideline operation helped pay the bills, but I found myself in a position I didn't like: premature diversification had resulted in profits that did not justify the return on invested time. Fly-Clean would never "fly" if I continued to play Hinton the Hobbyist!

FLYERS ALL

My corporate baby was three years old and had grown in awkward spurts. Fly-Clean's customer list expanded considerably during that time, much to my relief. Its history, however wobbly, gave me something to look back on so I could see how far I had come.

When the work load got heavy in the field, I hired and trained a part-time crew to work with me. The paperwork, however, piled up like soap suds. I really needed a secretary—someone to type invoices, write checks, and answer the phone. I was busy making sales calls, ordering supplies, and washing airplanes.

I couldn't afford to rent an office, so one of my spare bedrooms became Fly-Clean's headquarters. It was barely big enough for me and my desk—there was definitely no room for a secretary. Besides, I rather doubted that I could hire a quality person to work in my bedroom.

A friend of mine referred me to a lady who was an independent secretary and worked in her home. She lived near Sharpstown, and her location was easily accessible from the freeway. When I called her, she sounded warm, friendly, and professional over the phone—just what I wanted for Fly-Clean's image. I made an appointment to go see her.

————◆————

Wanda's kids were in high school and her husband was gone during the day. She had converted her dining room into an office; and yes, she could answer the phone with a "real voice," provided I could remember to forward it to her before I left my house. She agreed to schedule all the cleaning jobs and handle the billing. It looked like a perfect match to me.

I had never worked with a secretary before and she had never worked for a black boss. She grew up in a small country town between Houston and Austin where blacks were just "niggers," no matter what their status in the workplace. Wanda had not been contaminated by this outdated attitude, and seemed to realize that blacks and whites had many more similarities than differences.

The desire for personal growth was on Wanda's agenda as well as mine. We traded discoveries, and shared what worked and didn't work in our lives. Jonathan Livingston Seagull, that lovable "flyer" in Richard Bach's best-selling book, was my hero of the day, and I constantly referred to the essence of the story.

"Wanda, all you got to do when things overwhelm you in life is just fly a little bit higher, like Jonathan," I encouraged. "It gets lonesome when you choose to be different than the rest of the gulls, but it doesn't have anything to do with being right or wrong—it just means you're different. You have to be true to yourself, that's all," I preached joyously.

"Yeah, you're different, all right," she laughingly reminded.

"I know," I chuckled. "I always have been. Even as a kid, I was different. I always felt like an outcast in my

own community because of what Big Girl did for a livin'.
Then I went to a white school and felt different 'cause I
was black. But when I got to Baltimore, I realized there
wasn't no black and white issue—it was a *people* issue.
The Poles didn't get along with the Jews; the Italians
didn't get along with the Puerto Ricans; and I realized no
matter where I was or what I was doin', I definitely was
different. I didn't think of myself as black or *any* color for
that matter—I was just me, Eddie Hinton."

"Well," Wanda sighed, "you've certainly lived a different lifestyle than most of us," she acknowledged. "Most
people just talk about enjoying life. But you? You just do
it!" she said admirably.

————◆————

Wanda had several clients besides me. She also provided secretarial services to a woman whose husband was
Chuck Sims. Chuck was a true entrepreneur. He started
his company called "Remco" with one television rental
store, and it had become one of the largest rent-to-own
chains in America. Chuck attributed the success of Remco
to good strategic planning. I was invited to a private planning session at their ranch in the country.

Meetings of any kind were still pretty boring to me, but
this was too good an opportunity to pass up. I felt it was
an honor to get to spend two days with Chuck. When I
walked into the main house at the ranch, I knew he knew
how to produce results. It was also obvious to me he was a
"flyer" like Jonathan Livingston Seagull.

He was dressed in jeans and cowboy boots and seemed
to be almost six feet tall. His hands were the broadest I
had ever seen outside the football stadium, and he used
them to emphasize each important point. Chuck was in-
tensely focused on the purpose of the meeting, and I could

easily imagine him at the helm of a company. I had a feeling we wouldn't be wasting much time on small talk.

Chuck started the planning meeting with a series of questions about my business, and then he took me on a search for the answers. We came to a part in the process where Chuck asked me to state the exact purpose of Fly-Clean. I relaxed a little bit, thinking it was going to be easy.

"That's easy, Chuck. The purpose of Fly-Clean is to clean airplanes," I shrugged simplistically.

"Yes, but you also clean buildings and parking lots and oil rigs and buses and mobile homes," he said as he tallied on his fingers impatiently. "So that purpose doesn't exactly fit. Let me ask you again . . . what's the purpose of Fly-Clean?" Chuck walked restlessly around the room while I contemplated the question again. I made several attempts at putting my purpose into words, feeling somewhat foolish that it seemed so difficult. Finally, I felt like I had it.

"The purpose of Fly-Clean is to be an industrial cleaning company," I stated with conviction.

"Good, Eddie! That's clear," he said, grinning ever so slightly. "Now, how large do you want the company to be?" Chuck asked abruptly. "Think about it while I get some tea," he instructed as he walked towards the kitchen. "You want anything?" he yelled back pleasantly, remembering his Southern hospitality.

"No, thanks," I hollered. I had enough to swish around! It was scary answering this one.

When Chuck came back in the room, I spewed out my answer loud and clear before I lost my courage.

"The purpose of Fly-Clean is to be the largest industrial cleaning company in the world," I said, and waited for his reaction.

He sipped his tea, frowned into his cup as if reading the leaves, and then challenged me again. "Eddie, that's kind of ridiculous—let's just say in the Houston metropolitan area."

"Naw, Chuck. It can happen!" I argued, unwilling to give up my exciting new vision. "It's a service business . . . it can happen!"

"Well, how are you going to get there?" he countered. "The track record that you're showing now . . . well, based on that, you're not going to make it."

"I'm learnin' as fast as I can," I laughed, trying to cover the truth and timeliness of his words. "Shouldn't I know the answer to that question by the end of this plannin' session?" I asked, facetiously.

On and on the drills went. For two grueling days, it was focus, focus, focus. My respect for Chuck's accomplishments increased by the hour. He was the most disciplined thinker I had ever met. Chuck's mandate was: "State clearly what you want and what it's going to take to get there. What are your objectives? What are the steps you must take to achieve them?"

Thankfully, he kept at me until I was able to state the vision that was lurking in my head. The planning we had done suddenly seemed easy compared to what it was going to take to turn it into reality.

———◆———

"Wanda . . . this is Eddie . . . sorry to call so late, but ah . . . well, I just got a call from Oklahoma and I'm gonna have to run up there early in the mornin' . . . Well, Big Girl had a stroke and wrecked her car just as she was drivin' into the garage and she's in a coma in the hospital . . . No, I don't know how bad she's hurt; not too bad, I don't think . . . but the stroke . . . well, they just don't know yet what the situation is . . . No, I may be gone three or four days . . . it just depends on what I find out when I get there . . . Yeah, if you can just keep things rollin' with the crew and keep the invoices typed up and sent out . . . No, I'm gonna fly, just in case I have to bring a car back . . . I don't know what I'll be facin' or how long . . . yeah, Bubba's food is in the utility closet over the dryer . . . about 4 cups every mornin' . . . and could you get the mail while you're there? . . . Okay . . . yeah, I'll call you soon as I know somethin', and you have that number up there in case you need me . . . right . . . Thanks . . . I appreciate that . . . I'll call. . . ."

I don't know what I would have done without Wanda. She was always there when a crisis came up. I knew she would handle everything in my absence, including washing the towels we used to dry the airplanes. We had become like brother and sister, and she would be standing by for further word about Big Girl.

The airplane droned effortlessly through the cloudless April sky. Walter's question of long ago kept surfacing in my thoughts. "What we gonna do if she dies?" he had asked in bewilderment so many years ago. I tried not to think about the answer this time.

Instinctively, I knew it would be up to me to handle Big Girl's affairs. I had to set my emotions aside and concentrate on matters of business. If she lived, I would have to hire a nurse to live with her. I knew she would never move to Houston, and I knew for certain I wasn't going to live in Lawton. If she died, what would happen to the house, the furniture, the car? Who was going to pay the expenses?

———◆———

Big Girl's house looked strangely large without her in it. Even the jukebox seemed to be keeping a silent vigil. Her mail was stacked on the kitchen counter and the telephone receiver was sticky in my hand as I dialed the hospital.

The doctors still didn't know much. There were no serious injuries from the collision, but since she was still in a coma, they couldn't gauge the extent of the stroke damage. It didn't look good, though, they had gently warned.

I could visit her in intensive care, but the only indication that she knew I was in the room came from the heart monitor. The lines on the screen told me there was recognition somewhere deep within her consciousness. All I could do during the waiting was hold her hand and whisper, "Big Girl, it's up to you and Big Fella."

When I wasn't at the hospital, I shut myself in her bedroom and sorted her papers, trying to figure out what was what. Friends and creditors were already calling.

"I heard that your mother passed away and she owed us some money," they had said, accusingly.

"No, she's not dead as far as I know and I'll take care of her bills *if* and *when* the time comes," I had retorted angrily.

Early the fourth morning, I got the call from the hospital.

"Mr. Hinton, you better come."

At 6:45 that morning, I was standing next to her bed holding her hand. She was breathing irregularly, and all of a sudden she stopped. She was gone, just like that! The only thing that came to my unregistering mind was "Look how quickly life can go!"

It was the first time I had ever been close to the experience of death, and the chubby face of a little black boy with taps on his shoes floated through my memory. I loved Big Girl dearly and I knew she had only stepped into the invisible side of life. I concentrated on that thought to keep from weeping. There would be a time for tears, but now I had to go to work. There was a funeral to arrange and family to deal with.

———◆———

Dad had been retired from the Army for almost ten years, and while I was at the University of Oklahoma, he had moved from Lawton to Fort Worth, Texas. He and Big Girl had continued to see each other over the years, in spite of their geographical separation.

He had a small house, a job as head waiter at a local country club, and my two brothers lived with him most of the time. Walter was in his early thirties and Reggie was almost eighteen. Walter and Reggie stayed in the background, much as they always had when I was present. Except for occasional questions about the arrangements, they left matters up to me.

There was a service for Big Girl at the church and I had requested a short, simple eulogy. I put her house on the market immediately, and most of her personal items were donated to charity. I had done what I knew had to be done, and I returned to Houston once again. I was not proud that there had been no tears from her number one son. They just would not come, although my heart was in mourning.

———◆———

My desk was covered with small stacks of papers, notes, and bills. It was dusky in the office; the slats of the mini-blinds squeezed tightly against the afternoon sun.

I reached for the phone to call Big Girl. She'd be excited when I told her my picture was in the paper again! Just as my hand touched the receiver, I remembered. *Big Girl's dead now. Two months already. How could you forget?*

The moan escaped before I could stop it. "Oh, Big Girl . . . Mama . . . I miss you so much!"

The salty drops gushed over the dams of my eyelids and ran down my cheeks. The torrential tears would not be stopped, so I laid my head on top of the desk debris and clenched the phone for support.

22

HOLD THAT LINE

The phone rang like a trainman's alarm clock and my tear-salted eyes opened to darkness. The outstretched arm on the desk belonged to me, even though I couldn't feel it. In my semi-sleep state, I wondered if it was Big Girl calling *me*. I rubbed my eyes and lifted the insistent receiver.

"Eddie Hinton speaking."

"Hello, Eddie. This is Bob Watson," the unfamiliar but friendly voice said. "I play for the Houston Astros," he added, noncommittally.

"Oh, yeah . . . I've heard your name a time or two. How's it goin'?" I asked, trying to picture his face. We had met someplace before, but I was too groggy to remember where.

"Goin' great! How 'bout you?" Bob asked politely.

"Well, so-so." I answered truthfully. "Business is pretty good right now, and seems to be pickin' up."

"Glad to hear it!" he said sincerely. "That's mainly what I called about. I belong to a men's breakfast club called The Whitehall Club. I've been going there three years now. We meet every Friday morning at 7:15 out at River Oaks Country Club. Know where that is?" he asked.

"Sure, I've been out there." I said, slightly impatient. My arm was waking up and I tried to shake the tingles out of it.

"Like I said, I'm a member, but I'm going to be moving out of Houston next month. I was wondering if you would be interested in replacing me," he said hopefully.

"Well, that does sound kinda' interestin'," I said as I stretched some kinks out of my arm. "Tell me more about it. Who are these people and what do they do?" I quizzed.

"Oh, I'd say there's between sixty and seventy guys who attend on a regular basis. We exchange ideas and business leads with each other while we have breakfast. We also have a speaker at almost every meeting—either someone from the club or we invite someone from outside to present new ideas to the group," he explained.

"Do you have to pay to belong?" I asked cautiously.

"Yeah, we each put in fifty bucks a month to cover some of the expenses," he answered. "These men are pros," he assured me. "We try to get a member from each business and professional category. You can represent the aircraft cleaning business. I don't think they have one of those!" he laughed.

"No, probably not, 'cause I seem to be the only one in Houston—the only one that's mobile, that is," I stipulated humorously. "Well, just off the top of my head, I'd say yeah, I'm interested. What would be the next step?" I asked.

Bob and I made plans to meet for lunch the next day. My stomach growled like a hidden animal that had been awakened by the aroma of food.

———◆———

Bob had been an Astros first baseman for over ten years and would soon be on his way to Atlanta to continue his professional career with the Braves. He was invited to be a member of The Whitehall Club primarily because of his business investments. It certainly didn't hurt that he was a professional athlete.

"You know, Bob," I mused, as I finished my salad, "Big Fella's always watchin' out for me. I've been strugglin' along with Fly-Clean for five years now. My success has been based on trial and error . . . try somethin', and if that don't work, try somethin' else. It's gonna be wonderful to have a soundin' board and the opportunity to open some new doors in the community. But I'm curious . . . why did you pick me to replace you at The Whitehall Club?"

"Oh, I did some checking around the city and your name kept coming up. People said good things about you and Fly-Clean, so I figured you were good enough to replace me," he grinned.

"Well, it's an honor to be asked and I'm lookin' forward to networkin' with the members. Hope there's a marketin' expert whose brain I can pick! I'm tellin' you—I've tried every promotion I can think of for Fly-Clean. I've printed brochures, ran sales, baked brownies, visited every airport in the city, changed the color of my trucks, put uniforms and hats on my crew—you name it—I've done it!" I expounded.

"These guys are so helpful, Eddie," he said respectfully. "They understand what you're going through, because they've been there. When we go to the meetings, we're there to share. It's serious business most of the time, but they share a few jokes, too," he confided, chuckling.

"Well, I wish there would have been a Whitehall Club when I got out of football," I sighed. "I didn't know a financial statement from a jockstrap, and before I knew it, I was up to my shoulder pads in debt."

"I know what you mean, man. It's a jungle out there if you don't know what you're doing," Bob sympathized. It sounded like he had been there, too!

———◆———

Through the networking activities of The Whitehall Club, I had an opportunity to bid on a long-term contract to wash, wax, and detail a DC-8 for a private oil company. When the job was awarded to Fly-Clean, it was another milestone in the company's growth. It was the first time the bottom line came up profit instead of loss.

23

MEET CASH TAYLOR

Watching others prepare for Christmas was not my favorite holiday sport. Surely there was something I could do to move out of my depressed state of mind to at least a civil "Bah, Humbug"! This was the second Christmas without Big Girl, and even though we seldom celebrated the event together, I seemed to miss her most on that day.

When I least expected it, that voice inside me sent its own Christmas message. *Do something new, Eddie! Look for a challenge. Blaze a new trail. Count your blessings and stop feeling sorry for yourself. You've got a lot to be thankful for!*

As penance for my unusually lousy attitude, I made a list of everything I had to be thankful for. When it was complete, I realized anew that I was indeed abundantly blessed. I had a house, a car, plenty of food to eat, and the bottom line of Fly-Clean was no longer written in red ink. A little black kid from Oklahoma had entered, survived, and was prospering in the free enterprise system. I decided to join in the spirit of the season by rewarding myself with a long-awaited Christmas present.

◆

The "Horses for Sale" section of the newspaper had looked promising, but after several weeks of searching, I was somewhat discouraged. I had not found my dream horse yet. The ad I had called about sounded exciting. As I drove into the muddy, rutted drive in Northeast Houston, a smile crossed my face. The shabby stables reminded me of the OK Corral, and so did the aroma that quickly permeated the cab of my truck.

A young woman with a feed bucket came out of a small, rickety shed and limped toward my truck.

"Howdy. You must be Eddie."

"Right, and you must be Karen," I greeted. She was a somber little gal, I'd guess around twenty years old. Her straight, brownish hair was windblown and she wore no makeup to hide the traces of pain in her face. "Nice to meet you, Karen. What happened to your leg?" I asked with bold concern.

"Fell off one of my horses goin' around a barrel," she explained. "Tore up my knee and had to have it operated on. Doctor told me to wear this brace for six months, so I won't be ridin' for awhile," she said with remorse. "That's why I've got to sell my horses. Can't afford to feed 'em and not ride 'em," she said solemnly. "They're all gone, now, 'cept for Cash." She put the bucket down and zipped up her windbreaker.

"Sorry to hear about your leg," I said, feeling her emotional pain. "Sure hope it heals up okay. Them injuries ain't no fun!" I said severely. "I been there."

"Do you want to ride him?" she asked, ignoring my comment. "He ain't been ridden in 'bout two weeks. Prob'ly kinda skittish. This cold snap don't help none, either," she said, rubbing and blowing on her hands to warm them. "It's awful muddy in the arena, but you could stay on the edges." Karen limped toward the stall and I followed, offering to help saddle him.

The horse started to fidget as we approached, sensing something more exciting than the oats in Karen's bucket. He was a beautiful rusty-red color and his muscle tone was good. His socks and feet were black, and he had a patch of white abstract artwork between his eyes.

Karen reached for a halter from a nearby hook. "His full name's Cash Taylor. He's got good blood lines and his papers are on the seat of my truck," she reported as if following a checklist.

Cash was eager to get outside and tossed his head friskily at Karen. "Whoa, Cash. Take it easy, boy," she soothed.

He definitely had a lot of energy. Putting his saddle on was no easy chore. I helped as much as I could, and tried not to get in her way.

Karen was patient with both of us. "He's just excited 'cause you're a stranger," she said apologetically, "and, like I said, he ain't been ridden in a while."

"That's okay. I can handle him. I've been ridin' since I was a little kid in Oklahoma." I wrapped the reins around my hand, thankful that I'd worn leather gloves. Staying on this guy in the cold, muddy arena was going to be a challenge. He was definitely anxious to stretch his legs.

My attention was totally on Cash as I hefted my 200 pounds into the saddle. I could tell there would be an intense struggle to see which one of us was boss. My muscled thighs gripped tightly as I reined him in a controlled walk around the slick, mushy arena. Gradually, I eased him into a trot, then a canter and finally a gallop. He possessed the flamboyant spirit I had looked for but had not found in other candidates, and I could tell right away we were going to be able to communicate.

We were both sweating by the end of the trial ride. Karen opened the arena gate and Cash reluctantly turned toward his stall. Mud had splattered on his flanks and neck, and I offered to clean him up. It would be the polite thing to do, and would also be a good way to examine him more thoroughly.

"How soon could I pick him up if I give you a check today?" I asked when I finished grooming him and reading his papers. My decision was made and I was anxious to get acquainted with Cash.

"Well, anytime's fine with me," she said cooperatively. "You got a trailer?"

"No, but I've got a friend I can borrow one from. He lives out near Brookshire." How long had I dreamed about this moment? "Would Tuesday be all right?" I asked eagerly.

"Sure. Just come on out after lunch. You got a place to keep him?" she asked, obviously concerned.

"Well . . . no, not yet," I replied hesitantly. "But my friend Clifford Ray lives near Richmond and he's got a few acres and a barn." I brightened at my new brainstorm. "I'm positive Clifford will let me keep him there. I'll have to go out and feed Cash everyday, but that way I'll get to ride him a lot," I replied.

Karen's face clouded momentarily, then she continued even more soberly. "He's had most of his shots, but it's time to worm him again. And he'll need to be shoed before you ride him much. I'll write down his special brand of feed, and you can prob'ly get his vitamins at any tack or feed store," she informed.

Karen's invisible list kept getting longer and longer! "Special food? Vitamins? This horse is gonna live better than me!" I joked, knowing it wasn't far from the truth.

———◆———

Cash Taylor moved out of Karen's stall and into my heart. There were horse books to read and horseshoes to buy, but I still had business appointments to keep, too. My

daily routine expanded to include two extra hours with
Cash in order to train and care for him.

It was strange, but the horse seemed to have a personality just like mine—excitable, unpredictable, competitive,
obstinate, and lovable. He was also smart, responsive,
and a little bit wild—just what I'd always dreamed he
would be.

24

BACK TO THE TURF

Cash Taylor didn't get along very well with the horses on the other side of Clifford's pasture fence, so after a few months, it was necessary to find him a new home and a babysitter.

The Great Southwest Equestrian Center was located about six miles west of Houston and a few miles south of Katy. I wandered around the facility for almost half an hour, then came across a small building that looked like an office near the indoor arena. There was a pert little gal who seemed to be in charge, so I introduced myself to her. When I asked Kay for information about stall rentals, she politely offered to get someone else, because she was the polo instructor. She must have thought I was rude for gaping at her so dumbfoundedly! I couldn't believe my ears! She had said polo instructor!

Now, most people would say a black guy from Oklahoma who yearned to play polo had to be crazy. I agreed totally with that supposition, but it was a crazy dream I had had since childhood. At Ft. Sill's Museum in Lawton, the only interest I had as a kid was in the polo displays. It was there I learned that cavalry riders trained and exercised their own horses in polo matches. When I first

moved to Houston to play for the Oilers, I heard about the
Houston Polo Club. On Sunday mornings, I would go
watch the team practice, enthralled by the thunderous action. I was so excited at meeting Kay, I couldn't think of
which question to ask first.

———◆———

We had been sitting in the shade of the empty arena for
almost an hour. Kay was explaining the differences between outdoor polo and arena polo, a new indoor version
of the "game of kings."

". . . and arena polo is played with three people to a
team. The field of play is about one-third the size of outdoor polo. The rubber ball is bigger too, so it's easier to
see in the dirt and it doesn't travel quite as fast as the small
bamboo or plastic ball used on grass. The rules are a little
different, but basically, it's the same—just a scaled down
version of the outdoor game. So when would you like to
start your lessons?" she grinned expectantly.

I started to say, "Oh, about 25 years ago." Instead I answered, "Well, how about next Saturday? I'll have to borrow a trailer to get my horse out here."

"Is he a thoroughbred?" she asked. "Thoroughbreds
make the best polo ponies, you know."

My heart sank. *I finally get my dream horse, finally find
a place to take polo lessons, and now I find out I've got
the wrong kind of horse? Gimme a break, lady,* I thought
unkindly.

"How come they only use thoroughbreds?" I asked, already trying to figure a way around this obstacle.

"Because thoroughbreds have more stamina and instinct
for the game. You run a horse up and down a 300-yard
field for seven and a half minutes in the hot sun—they
have to be strong. You switch mounts after every chukker,
which is similar to quarters in football," she explained,

"but in polo, there's six chukkers in an outdoor match. That's why it takes a minimum of three good horses to play."

I groaned inside. *A minimum of three thoroughbreds. Go for it, Hinton.*

"Uh . . . Cash is a quarterhorse," I said ruefully, "but he's real smart, and I work him a lot, so he's well-muscled. He ain't no sissy," I added in his defense. "I could at least take lessons on him, couldn't I? We'll be usin' the indoor arena, won't we? He won't get too tired." I had to convince her somehow.

Since they were trying to encourage business at the new center, she told me it would be okay for me to use Cash, but if I was ever going to play seriously, I'd have to get better horses . . . a minimum of three.

I couldn't imagine cleaning triplet stalls, even if the residents *were* thoroughbreds.

———◆———

The excitement and enthusiasm I felt during the first polo practice was much greater than I could have imagined. After being out of professional football for eleven years, I finally found something to replace the level of competitiveness that had eluded me, even in the world of business.

Polo had all the ingredients I was looking for. It required instant reactions and superb balance both from the rider and mount. The rules of the game were made to protect the horse, so the rider was inherently responsible for something other than himself. Polo instantly captured my heart, mind, body, and soul.

———◆———

Because I already knew how to ride, I went to the side-lines of the polo class. While the rest of the group practiced their horsemanship, I looked for diversions until we could all play together as a team. That's when I discovered "cutting and roping," an age-old skill of the early cowboy.

After several months of hanging around the Center, I discovered that there were invisible barriers, even in this arena of sports. Horse lovers were also afflicted with the "people issue"! I had to laugh at the ridiculousness of the human family in spite of the twinge of sadness I felt within. *When will we learn to love one another?*

Instead of waiting around for that glorious day, I decided to learn to rope one of them cows!

25

THE CORPORATE COIN TOSS

The oil crunch of the mid-80's dropped a loop around the horns of Texas and brought it to the ground. Luxuries, such as corporate and private aircraft, were dropped from budgets as the price of oil plummeted.

Fly-Clean had to struggle to pay its creditors and survive. I was up to my neck in personal debt and doubt. That familiar voice inside me nagged constantly, as it always would at times like these. *Maybe you should give the business up. Maybe you should go work for someone else. Maybe you're not gonna make it this time.* But its unwelcome suggestions held no charm for me—I loved my independence too much. I'd worked too hard to let it slip away. Besides, it might look like failure; and that was totally unacceptable to me as long as I could still do something about it. There were people out there depending on me: creditors, employees, and other athletes who would follow my path from the locker room to the boardroom.

———◆———

Whenever I got stuck and didn't know which way to go, I always reverted to what I'd learned playing football. I searched my mental files for some answers. *What am I not doing? Where am I off track? How can I make this work?*

Then one day it dawned on me. I didn't have any team-mates on my team. I was the owner, the quarterback, the runner, the tackler, the head coach, and water boy—one person doing all the jobs. I was at that critical stage Chuck had talked about in the planning session: Fly-Clean's growth had carried me downfield toward the goal line, but it had also placed me in a precarious predicament. It was no longer a one-person operation, and for the next level of organizational activity, I needed marketing, financial, and industry expertise. So I began to ask myself how I could form a team.

The Chamber of Commerce gave me names of compa-nies in aviation who could help me. Through the various phone calls and networking systems in Houston, the per-fect people showed up on my doorstep. One guy was a former owner of a charter service. Another guy had thirty years experience in aviation. Suddenly, because I was looking, I had an abundance of talented people who wanted to be on my team. It wasn't quite so lonely any-more even though the ultimate responsibility for the score still rested on my shoulders.

——◆——

We huddled. We drilled. We brainstormed.

What came out of our meetings were possibilities for the future. Fly-Clean had a uniquely designed product, a plan, and a team. Franchising was one of our goals, be-cause it would allow us to help others duplicate our suc-cess. We could raise the money by selling stock, either privately or publicly. After extensive research, the corpo-rate coin was tossed, and it came up "public."

When Fly-Clean's "penny" stock appeared for over-the-counter trading, it sold 4 million units of stock and warrants at 5 cents per unit in less than a week.

PART THREE

. . . and that the only time that matters is today.

. . . Kendrick Mercer

26

WELCOME TO THE REAL WORLD

The glow-in-the dark dial on my clock radio said it was shortly after midnight. So why was the phone ringing so incessantly, I wondered, as I rolled over to strangle it.

"Hullo," I mumbled as my eyelids fought against the intrusion.

"Eddie, this is Anthony."

"Anth . . ."

"Anthony Hutchison! I'm in New York," he said.

My memory began its sleepy search to find "Hutchison, Anthony" in one of its files. There—that's the one: Anthony was 26 years old and had been playing professional football for over three years. During that time, his life had been like a roller coaster ride. He played, got cut, then his contract was picked up by Buffalo for a pre-season. He was a saucy kid with a million-dollar grin, and his delicate ebony face always looked like it had been scrubbed and polished. He was 5′10″, and had the chiseled physique of an Olympian. Anthony had spent most of his teenaged years at a boys home in San Antonio. We had met at a party in Houston and he promptly adopted me as his mentor.

"I know it's late, hom'," Anthony was saying, "but I had to talk to somebody. You awake?" he asked desperately.

"Yeah, man . . . it's okay . . . go ahead . . . what's. . . ."

"I got cut today," he said with familiar anguish in his voice. His statement brought me out of sleep and into the reality of the middle of the night.

"Hey, man, that's bad news," I sympathized. "What are you gonna do?"

"Well, I'm comin' back to Houston as soon as I get things wrapped up here," he sighed. "I should be back sometime next week."

"Gimme a holler when you get to town—is there anything I can do in the meantime?" I asked. I remembered well going over that same cliff some ten years earlier. This was his second time around, but you never get used to it.

"No, E. G.—well, yeah, on second thought, there is somethin' you can do. I'm gonna need a good banker when I get to Houston—you know any?"

"Sure do, but you can't call him tonight," I laughed sleepily. "As soon as you get back in town, I'll take you down and introduce you to Lloyd."

"Okay, E. G. I'll call you as soon as I get in. Sorry I woke you up," he said humbly, "and thanks for listenin'."

———◆———

The conference room was subtle elegance—chandeliers, marshmallow carpet, and polished mahogany. Lloyd, my banker, was all smiles as he ushered us to padded chairs. He was a distinguished looking businessman and always seemed at home in his navy pin-striped suit. Lloyd had been my banker for years, and had seen me through the hard times. It just so happened I had a deposit to make, but I wanted Anthony to tell Lloyd his story first.

Anthony got paid well, if and when he was playing. To make ends meet while waiting around for another team to hire him, he had decided to start a landscaping company in Houston.

When Anthony finished making his request, I placed the deposit envelope on the table in front of Lloyd and turned to Anthony.

"Anthony, the only reason we're sittin' here today is because this banker has seen me go through the struggle of operatin' a business. The only reason he's talkin' to me now is 'cause I got money. Don't fool yourself into thinkin' that it's because I'm a nice guy. Business doesn't work that way."

The room was quiet and Anthony was all ears. I continued in order to make my point.

"The reality of it all is you have to bust your butt and work smart, whether you're on the football field or in the business world. People love to surround themselves with successful people, and at this moment, Lloyd thinks I'm very successful as evidenced by what's in that envelope. Now Lloyd, why don't you tell Anthony how a banker looks at professional athletes?" Lloyd was used to my strange requests, and he also knew me well enough to know that I wanted him to speak the truth.

He cleared his throat, and looked at Anthony. "Well, Anthony, I can't speak for every banker in this city, but around here, we don't think very highly of dealing with athletes. We'll only loan money if it's collateralized because our impression from the media is that most of you are on drugs anyway." Lloyd didn't pull any punches.

I turned to a disbelieving Anthony and tried to explain further. "See, you have a tough hurdle to clear. People are gonna think whatever they think, no matter who you are or what you do. I'm guessin' the only reason you're gonna be able to do business with this banker, is because of my personal recommendation. The only reason I'm sharin'

this information with you, Anthony, is because I've been
where you are now. Did anybody ever teach you how
banks work or why it's important to maintain a good relationship with a bank?" I asked.

Anthony shook his head.

"Well, me neither!"

I had known Anthony for just a short time, but my gut
confirmed that he was okay. He was determined to make
it, and *would* make it, no matter what!

I looked at Lloyd and said, "I believe Anthony is like a
junkyard dog . . . I'd bet on him!" Then I turned to Anthony and said, "The only reason this banker's gonna deal
with you is because of what I just said. So don't let yourself down."

———◆———

Anthony was quiet on the ride back to the office. Traffic
kept me busy while his situation spoke to my heart. I felt a
rage inside, and reminisced about my own experiences.

Before a pro contract is signed, there's plenty of people
to give you advice and they stand in line for your money.
Once the ink is dry, however, you're pretty much alone,
unless you happen to be a superstar. Superstars are very
rare, but they're always surrounded by people—all kinds
of people.

Where are all these "advisors" when they're really
needed? They're back in line waiting for the new crop. I
thought about the familiar stories told by athletes—how
so-called "relatives" crawl out from under the brush like
serpents when they sense money in the offing; or how relationships are shattered by the lifestyle, the tension, and
the uncertainty; or how egos get destroyed by people who
are paid to tell you "sorry, you're not good enough anymore"; or how financial futures are sucked away by peo-

ple of questionable integrity who say "have I got a deal for you!"

What happens when the Anthonys can't play? How did all these people manage before athletes got paid for their talent? How come there is no support system? What about the future of the athlete? Who will help him in business when times get *really* tough?

Fly-Clean had allowed me to create networks of assistance, but the process had taken years. Many, many people gave me free advice, volunteer labor, and encouraging words. Now I could begin to repay their kindness by helping those at the edge of the chasm.

Athletes are special people with extraordinary discipline. They have gigantic egos, yet fragile self-esteem. Most of us rely heavily on intuition, but rarely is this gift balanced by practical reality.

When athletes can transfer physical accomplishments into lifelong economic freedom, we will have made our fullest contribution to the system. Until we do, our short-term greatness (and long-term dependency) is one of the biggest hazards of the game.

No one puts us at the bottom of the chasm—we just step off the unseen cliff, blindfolded by our own lack of information, education, and imagination. If we try to blame others, we only add to the slime that coats the steep walls.

What we *can* do is erect warning signs, prepare road maps, and train each other in the ways of success. We can build cement handholds out of the chasm, or we can build bridges across it. We can utilize our God-given talents by guiding those who follow our footsteps.

Once again, that voice inspired me: *We must not lose any more great, young athletes to the deep, dark chasm.*

27

THE GOLDEN RULE BOOK

It was several days before I heard from Anthony again. When I answered his call, he was already talking full speed.

"Eddie, I don't know what to do . . . Buffalo called me back to play . . . can you believe that? Do you think I should go? What would you do?"

"Whoa, there boy! Slow down a little bit, or are they waitin' on the other line for your answer?" I chuckled.

"No man . . . I'm just excited . . ." he laughed, "so anyway, E. G., what would you do?" he asked, a note of seriousness creeping into his voice.

"That's difficult, Anthony. You have to search your soul and answer the question, 'What will make me happy?' I can't answer that for you—only you can. It's your life."

"Oh, man! Why do you think I called you? I wanted you to give me an answer!"

"I just gave you my answer," I said gently.

"Yeah, I guess you did," he sighed. "Well . . . I guess I'll just have to . . . I've got 'til Wednesday to let 'em know. I'll just have to think on it some more. By the way, I really appreciate you introducin' me to Lloyd."

"You're welcome—glad to do it." I thought a minute. "Tell you what, Anthony. I'm drivin' to Oklahoma for the Sooners' game this weekend—you wanna go?"

"Sure do!" he exclaimed with excitement. "Let me check my work schedule just to be sure, but I think I'm clear. I'll call you back by noon."

———◆———

We settled into the four-lane highway, having survived the notorious Friday night traffic on its way out of Houston for weekend fun. Diana Ross was on my tape deck, Anthony was sipping an Orange Crush, and I was watching for highway patrol cars.

"You know man, I just don't know what to do," Anthony said as he turned down the volume a little. "If I go back to football, I'll have to give up the landscape company idea and move again or try to keep two houses. Who knows how long I might get to play? One game—forty? 'Course, football's what I know best and the money's decent, when I get to play. But if I don't go back, then the future's *totally* up to me. My business can make it, I think, if I just keep at it long enough."

No doubt about it—Anthony had a tough decision to make. "Yeah, hom', it's gonna be up to you *either* way you go, but I know what you mean. I've been in business a long time and I still feel like a rookie," I laughed.

"Well, it ought to be smooth sailin' for you, now that you've gone public."

"Oh, no, no, no," I corrected him. "It's almost like startin' over. It's a whole new ballgame! The rules have changed a little bit, but I know I have to keep on doin' the things I've been doin' 'til the clock runs out."

"Yeah? What things? Like what? What do you mean?" Anthony quizzed impatiently.

"Well, there's certain rules I play by, no matter what I'm doin'."

"Is it a secret code, or are you gonna tell me?" Anthony laughed, impatient for any suggestions that would help him. I pulled into the right lane so an 18-wheeler could pass. This kid really got to me. He was so eager to grow and learn; and he wanted so badly to be good . . . I could relate so well . . .

"Well, Anthony, I guess the first thing I do is decide what I want. Even when I was a kid, I was plannin' way in the future. Sometimes it was hard to find enough challenges to keep me goin', and sometimes people would try to detour me by sayin' things like, 'It can't be done' or 'think of others first' or 'it's not polite to ask for things.' Most people stumble through life like beggars with empty sacks, willin' to take whatever is handed out. Not me, hom'! I keep a picture of a Rolls Royce on my refrigerator so I see it everytime I open the door. Now, that don't mean I'm gonna run out and buy a Rolls the first time I have a spare dime, but it's a daily reminder that I can *do, be,* and *have* anything I want if I want it bad enough."

"Oh, you mean like positive thinkin'—that sorta thing?" he asked, genuinely perplexed.

"No, what I'm talkin' about is stronger than that even," I replied. "The Bible promises that anything we ask in His name shall be given, according to our faith."

"Hey, man, don't give me that! I've asked for things lotsa times and haven't gotten 'em. It don't always work!" he shot back with slight irritation.

"Maybe you didn't hear the key phrase in my statement—accordin' to our faith!" I reiterated. I decided to use Cash as an example to clarify my beliefs to Anthony. "Like when I was little and wanted a horse so bad, I got a football instead. But, you know what? I got my horse! I was just impatient! I got my horse 30 years later! It's still a miracle to me. If I'd had a horse when I was younger, I couldn't have taken care of it! I wouldn't have been able to take any lessons, and prob'ly would've screwed up a good horse! Cash Taylor came into my life at the perfect moment," I insisted. "I was just impatient for 30 years! Yes sir, I'm convinced—our heart's desire is what Big Fella truly wants for us. He didn't put us on this good earth to suffer—He put us here to learn and grow!" I preached, sounding like the old Reverend Jones from my childhood.

"Well, how do you do that? I mean . . . how do you know if you're growin' or not? I been bustin' myself to make it! Seems like somethin' is always holdin' me back. Sometimes, it seems like havin' a dream for the future is just . . . well, it's kinda like quicksand, man . . . the harder you squirm to get out, the more it sucks you back in," Anthony countered.

"Yeah, I know what you're talkin' about. Everytime I went back to Lawton I thought about how far I had come. And when I think about my mama . . . we called her Big Girl 'cause she was so obese . . . when I think about how far I've come compared to her and my Grandmother Odessa . . . well . . . I just have to thank Big Fella every day!"

Anthony was silent for a time. It had started to rain and the windshield wipers slapped out the beat of a half-time marching band. Boy, did I know what he was going through! But there would be more to come. He was still living in the dream world of pro athletes.

"How do you know when you've got the right answer?" Anthony asked. "Even if you *can* decide . . . how do you know?"

"Man, there ain't no guarantees! There ain't no security! I learned that big lesson in the oil crunch! Even the giants got hurt in that brawl! So you don't worry about bein' right—there ain't no such thing. You're gonna have regrets either way you go!" I predicted with certainty.

"What do you mean?" Anthony asked, perplexed by my remark.

"Well . . . let's see . . . take bein' single. Sometimes I have regrets about not bein' married and settled down and kids and dogs and all that stuff; but when I was married, I had regrets about not being single! See what I mean? Either way you go, there's gonna be regrets. So you just follow your heart," I said simply. "Like when I was in high school, I thought music was my heart's desire. But when my buddy, Byron, dropped out of music for football, I followed him to the field 'cause I looked up to him. Then football became a way to get an education and that was my heart's desire. Then when I was almost out of college, playin' with the pros became my heart's desire." I stopped to catch my breath. "I did a lot of soul-searchin' my first year at O.U. I used to sit in the dark in my room and stare out the window for hours wonderin', *What am I here for? What are my goals? Where am I goin'?* Then an answer finally came to me." I could feel Anthony watching me from his passenger seat, and I knew he had asked the same questions of himself.

"The answer was," I continued importantly, *Go use your talent and see where it takes you . . .* and that's what I been doin' ever since. I didn't get all the answers at once, but one answer led to the next step which led to the next question. It's an ongoin' process, man," I said with reverence.

Anthony thought about that for awhile. The oncoming lights bounced through the drops of rain on the windshield and dappled our shirts.

"You know, Eddie, sometimes I wake up in the middle of the night, scared to death." His voice was deeper, softer—almost as if he were confessing a sin.

"Yeah, I know . . . I been there, too," I said, without letting any sympathy slip in.

"Well, what did you do about fear? How did you handle that one?" he asked somberly.

"I ain't handled it yet, man . . . I'm still workin' on that one!" I laughed. "One thing I've noticed, though . . . it's always there! I guess I've learned to tuck it under my arm like a football, and just take it with me. Fear is the opposite of the faith we talked about. We can put our faith in God or we can put our faith in negative things like fear. Fear is false unless you make it come true. I'll take Big Fella any day."

"Well, how do you keep up your morale? It was easy for me when I was playin' and doin' a good job—it ain't so easy out here," Anthony admitted.

"I hear ya, man. But under the other arm, I tuck my self-esteem. And that's the way I go through life. If I'm not on my own team, who else is gonna be?" I asked, glancing at his handsome young profile. "There ain't no cheerleaders for us flyers. You and I *know* when we're doin' the very best job we can possibly do. That's all that matters," I assured him. "And if you make a mistake, you just correct it if you can and go on. A guy by the name of E. Hubbard once said, 'The greatest mistake you can make in life is to be continually fearing you will make one.'"

We both laughed at the simplistic wisdom. "Stop beatin' up on yourself, man," I mockingly pleaded. "You're whittlin' on your own finger! You ain't never a loser as long as you're playin' the game. There's always somethin' to learn, especially from mistakes!"

"Well, I'll probably make my share," Anthony confided.

"We all do, hom'," I consoled gently. "Just don't take it too serious . . . but if you're gonna play, you gotta know the rules. You gettin' hungry? Let's pull in up ahead and grab a burger."

28

THE PRICE OF THE TICKET

The cafe jukebox made me kind of homesick when I walked in. The linoleum on the floor even had a familiar crunch as we slid into a plastic booth. There weren't many people going north from the looks of the crowd—one leather-lined truck driver and a young couple sharing a shake. That made me kind of homesick, too.

We ordered twin burger baskets and orange juices, large. Our conversation turned to the O.U. game. We analyzed the players, the weather, and the possible effects of the weather on the game. The hamburgers, when they finally arrived, were lousy.

"No wonder there ain't many customers in here," I mumbled as we snatched toothpicks at the door and headed for the car.

Anthony offered to drive which fit my plans just fine—I would catch a little nap after supper. But Anthony had different ideas about what people do after meals. He was ready for another round since he had to stay awake anyway.

He adjusted the mirrors and successfully maneuvered the entrance to the highway. "So, after you decide what you want," he began, as if he'd never left the car, "and you've got fear under one arm and self-esteem under the other . . . then what do you do?" he grinned.

"You go for it," I said bluntly from my shotgun bed. "Whatever it is you want, go for it! Circumstances don't count."

"Could you explain that one?" he chuckled.

"Well, take me for instance. By all standards of logic, I should be fat, poor, uneducated, and dependent. I should have been counted out from the day I was born. But, whatever it took, I was not willin' for it to turn out that way! I still wear Big Girl's weddin' ring on my little finger to remind myself that I don't ever want to be fat like she was. When I was in college, I played with injuries so I wouldn't miss the opportunity of the pro scouts seein' me at the right time. I just turned a quarterhorse into a polo mount, which is a no-no. See what I mean? You don't let circumstances stop you."

"Yeah . . . yeah, I do. But how do you apply that to business? How do you make that work in Fly-Clean?" he asked.

"Well . . . I have to say . . . it took me three or four years just to get started, 'cause I was doin' everything myself. I had to keep the equipment working, and if the crew didn't show up, I had to do the jobs by myself. Sometimes, the weather was bad for weeks at a time, but I had to make a commitment to *keep* the business goin'!"

"What kind of commitment?" Anthony quizzed. "You mean financial?"

"For sure, financial!" I exclaimed. "But I guess you could say it was more like a vow. A friend of mine, Jan Bozarth, said it best: 'Commitment is a vow taken within my soul; a pledge of completion which represents a total faith in my ability to do the thing that has been promised and to do it without delay.' You know, Anthony, we've been trained to compete, and what that means to me is that I'm ready for any obstacles that might come up. In fact, I

love the challenge of usin' my mind to create a way! That
thrills me, man! It really excites me. I want to scream and
jump for joy when I know the challenge is there. It's *after*
I accomplish somethin' that I lose my steadiness! I don't
know where to go until I get somethin' else to go for!"

It was plain to see the nap would not be forthcoming. I
had talked myself right into excitement!

"You know, Anthony, as I look back over my life, it's
not the success that matters. It was the struggle, the tryin',
the process of achievement. Out of that process, I'm able
to see the growth within myself," I said in amazement.
"It's like when you're drivin' in the mountains. Sometimes, it looks like you're goin' downhill, but if you look
behind you, you can see you're in a steady climb."

"Well, I'm ready to get out of this valley I'm in," he
said disgustedly. "I guess I just need some new goals."

"Before you set any new goals, why don't you just
dream a little bit . . . get out there way in the future.
Think ahead of time." I chuckled as a memory popped
into my mind. "Like the game between O.U. and Notre
Dame. I fantasized about it for at least a year before it
happened. Then the picture got more real every time I
practiced that play. When the time came, I was ready, and
it worked!" I laughed. "So what do you want to be
doin'?" I asked, getting to the heart of the matter, "and
what are you willin' to pay to be doin' it?" I asked, seriously.

"What do you mean, 'pay to be doin' it'?" Anthony
asked, looking at me strangely.

"I have a plaque on my wall. In fact, I have several
plaques on my wall and Suenens' says, 'Happy are those
who dream dreams and are ready to pay the price to make
them come true.' That's what I mean," I emphasized.
"Nothin' is free, hom' . . . not even success. You pay a
price to play football. You pay a price to be in business.

You pay a price to be married. You pay a price to uphold your ideals."

"Yeah, like our people have paid a price," Anthony interjected.

"Yes, we have, hom', but the so-called "ticket-takers" in life have also paid dearly. Whether it's blacks or athletes or old folks or whatever, society loses when it has to take care of us. And what I'm sayin' is, potentially great *minds* are goin' to waste! No matter who we are, or what we do, or what our age might be; we can apply our talent, our knowledge and our discipline in any area we choose! The more we can do for ourselves, the more we can do for others! It's time to live in the present and the future, Anthony, not the past. If our global family will forgive each other and learn to cooperate and assist each other . . . well, it's just like football—there ain't any plays without assists. And there ain't gonna *be* a future if we don't all play on the same world team!" I croaked, caught up in my own idealism.

"That's true . . . it's such a small world and it's gettin' smaller every day. Global economy . . . changin' technology . . . there's so much knowledge I don't have yet," he said wistfully.

I could see my conversation was getting through to him.

"Well, you can't ever get enough. But, you see, there's a difference between knowledge and knowin' . . . knowledge comes through your head, and knowin' comes through your heart. You gotta be in tune with both."

"Like intuition? Is that what you're talkin' about?" he asked.

"Yeah . . . and instinct, too. Follow your instincts, man," I ordered gently. "I 'member when I was playin' in high school, I injured my leg. The coach wanted me to play anyway, but I just said 'Nope, ain't gonna play . . . 'cause I know if I do, I might be jeopardizin' my future!'

They didn't like it worth a hoot, but I knew!" I said, smacking the dashboard as if I had to convince him also.

Anthony was silent as we snaked our way over the surface of the blacktop. The rain had stopped, but clouds were still thick on the horizon. Occasional lightning brushed the night sky with pink-gold fairy flickers.

"When I got out of football, I was lookin' for a sales job," I laughed, reminiscing. "I was on an interview, talkin' to this sales manager guy. He had said, 'Well, Eddie, from the looks of your resume, you don't have much experience in selling.' I guess my life must've flashed before my eyes, 'cause I said, 'Well, you can't really go by that resume. I've been sellin' ever since I was in grade school—I've been sellin' myself to teammates, to coaches, and to my community all my life. I got so good at sellin', I sold myself to a scholarship at one of the largest universities in the country and it happened to be a football school in Oklahoma. I got my college degree and acknowledgment throughout the country for playin' the sport, then I sold myself to a professional team that decided to pay me money—prob'ly quite a bit more money than any salesman you've ever had. . . .' Boy, I'll tell you, he did a double-take at me, and next thing I knew, I was fillin' out a payroll form! It was so funny, how that happened. I guess I had to reach deep down inside and look at my basic experience. Heck, I figured if I succeeded once, I could do it again," I chuckled immodestly.

After Anthony stopped laughing, he dove in again.

"Do you feel like you've succeeded—lookin' back?" Anthony questioned.

"Oh, yeah! I've made a good livin', I've never missed a mortgage payment or went without a meal, and the learnin' has never stopped! I've been able to go to business seminars and workshops. I've done my job and got paid well," I said proudly. "One of the things I learned workin' for Mutual of New York was how to sell an intangible item to someone who thought they didn't want to buy it. It was a major steppin' stone for me, 'cause it proved I was capable of operatin' outside the physical arena. I learned to use my head for somethin' besides a target for somebody else's helmet!" I said.

"I hear ya, man," Anthony laughed. "Sometimes I think I must be crazy to want to go back out there."

"I guess I've been crazy about football since high school. I 'member one time in high school, I got a bad hip bruise and, macho man that I was, I tried to pretend it didn't bother me. Well, at practice, the coach saw I wasn't performin' 100%, and he ordered me to take five laps around the field. I told him, 'Coach, I can't do that—I've got a hip-pointer.' He yells at one of the other guys, 'Calvin, go in the dressing room and fetch me that paddle—I'll see if I can change Eddie's mind.' I said, 'Man, you must be CRAZY! I can't run—I can barely WALK!' He yells, 'CALVIN, GET OUT HERE WITH THAT PADDLE!' Well, I tore off my helmet and slammed it on the ground at his feet, ripped off my jersey and shoulder pads and slung 'em at the helmet. 'I QUIT! I'M THROUGH!' I said, and stomped off the field. I lasted two whole weeks and couldn't take it anymore. I didn't have nothin' to do—all my buddies were still on the team—and everybody kinda shunned me like I had a disease or somethin'."

"So what did you do?" Anthony asked in disbelief.

"I had to apologize to the coach and the team, then they let me come back. It was awful, man. It was the biggest chunk of pride I ever had to swallow, but I had to play the game. I had to go back. It was my identity, 'cause I didn't have any other. So, I know what you mean about wantin' to go back."

"And yet," Anthony said, struggling with his own conflict, "I want to go forward with my life. I want to have a little more control of my future. I want to try my skills in the business world—I want to learn somethin' and end up bein' somebody besides a broken down ex-jock," he admitted openly.

"Well, maybe you're like me, hom' . . . maybe you gotta do everythin' the hard way first."

"Yeah? Like what? What are you sayin' . . . intentionally make it hard? You gotta be crazy! I'm lookin' to *ease* the pain a little, not add to it," Anthony laughed.

"No, I'm not talkin' 'bout that . . . but . . . well, for instance, when I first started Fly-Clean, I thought my idea of a mobile cleanin' service was so great! But it just never occurred to me to have the business *at the airport!* Now that is dumb, man, *dumb!* So I go out and go through the agony of puttin' an idiot-proof machine together that can haul enough water to wash an airplane, but if I'd done it the easy way first, I wouldn't have a machine to sell now! So it all works out okay, but sometimes we put ourselves through the wringer—frontwards and backwards—just so we can learn."

"Whew! It makes you wonder sometimes! I know I've been tryin' and tryin' to put this landscape business together . . . guess it's just gonna take that extra mile," Anthony sighed.

"*Miles,*" I interrupted, "it's gonna take several," I assured him. "You can forget that second effort myth—sometimes it takes *hundreds*—you just make a commitment to yourself not to give up 'til you make it," I stated flatly.

"Ain't you got any good news, man?" Anthony laughed. He reached for another orange soda and I fumbled in my bag for another cassette. We still had a long way to go.

29

UNDER MY WING

The miles disappeared as Anthony and I traded war stories of our gridiron lifestyles—the pain, the glory, the glamour, and the emptiness. We talked about the greats and the unknowns and ended up at life after football again. It was easy to give advice from where I was, but Anthony was just beginning. I knew my answers would not be his answers, but I wanted him to know the truths I had discovered within myself. I wanted him to look inside his heart.

"So you got any suggestions about my business?" Anthony asked hopefully. "I mean, is there anything you see I'm not doin' that I should be doin'?"

"Well, Anthony . . . 'course I ain't been around your business much, but . . . well, I guess the best advice I can give is, no matter what it is you're gonna do, do your homework. Find out about the industry. Ask questions whenever you run into somebody who's willin' to share information," I suggested. "Focus on what it is you want, then go do it. I always tell people in advance what it is I'm gonna do, then I can't back out—I have to perform," I laughed boisterously. "Like when I knew I was gonna play Willie Brown—he played for Oakland at the time—

and he was the best bump-and-run cornerback in the AFC. When I was a rookie, I shot off my mouth and told the coaches I could beat him, and they just laughed and said, 'Shoot, he's No. 1.' Well, Willie only had a week to think about me when it came time to play, but I had a whole season to think about him. When the time came, I snagged five Unitas passes for 115 yards—the newspaper said I left Brown a physical wreck," I boasted slightly. "Now, that wouldn't have happened if I hadn't done my homework. Same thing with Fly-Clean. When I first started my business, there wasn't anyone to turn to for help, 'cause the concept was new. But after I explained it a few times, I was referred to people who could guide me, like pilots, mechanics, owners, salesmen—you name it— suddenly they were there," I said, still astounded by divine providence. "I met a guy named Johnny Ferry—I think he was an engineer or somethin'—and he was always tellin' jokes! One day he invited me to go to lunch and I almost turned him down 'cause I wasn't in a jokin' mood. Well, I went anyway and in the course of our conversation, I told him about the concept of Fly-Clean, and he said, 'You've got to come back to my office—I have something to show you.' Well, this guy reached in his drawer, pulled out a stack of pages and handed them to me. I thought I was gonna fall outta the chair when I saw that it was a business plan for a mobile cleanin' service! He told me to take it and use it however I wanted. He said he had gotten a lot of enjoyment out of watchin' me play, and it was his way of sayin' 'thanks.' Turns out, this guy is very creative, but he's not an implementor! So just for fun, he dreams up these ideas for businesses and then puts 'em in a drawer! His help was so timely . . . but the point is, even though I did everythin' the hard way, guys like him saved me time, money, and headaches. They helped me know what questions to ask. From there, it was up to me to find out what my job was," I said in summary.

"That's me right now . . . I'm not sure what my job is. When I'm playin' football, I know . . . but out here, well . . ."

"Don't get discouraged, Anthony—it'll come, it'll come," I reassured him. "I 'member my first year in the pros at Baltimore—I thought I was really hot stuff. I thought my job was to score! Well, after sittin' on the bench most of the season, it finally dawned on me. My job wasn't to score—my job was to catch the ball—just catch the ball! That's what they were payin' me for. After that finally sank in, it took some of the pressure off, and sometimes I scored and sometimes I didn't," I shrugged, indicating my compliance with the way life worked.

"Well, nobody's perfect, that's for sure," Anthony offered.

"Right, but it sure helps to know your job so well that you don't have to think—you can just react. I knew I'd made it as a pro when I got to that level," I explained.

"That's what a pro is, ain't it? Someone who's paid to do somethin' consistently well?" he asked proudly.

"You got it, hom'! You're on the right track!" I teased. I leaned back in the seat and closed my eyes, thinking of all the guys I played against—defensive opponents, they were called. Off the field, they were called friends. My mind drifted back to the long, hard practices before a big game. I had to laugh at how serious it had been at the time—life or death serious.

"What're you laughin' at, man?" Anthony asked curiously.

"Oh, I was just thinkin' back to some of the practices and how serious it all was. Jim Duncan, cornerback for the Colts . . . he was my practice partner. I mean, he was tough! He never let up on me an inch. In fact, if he thought I was doggin' it, he'd slap me up 'side the head and say, 'You better get with it, Hinton, or you'll be trade bait'—used to make me so mad, I'd get all fired up again, even if I was exhausted. Yeah, hom', I was real blessed . . . I got to play with and against winners through most of my career. Kept me at my best, even in practice! Winners give more than they take; losers take more than they give," I concluded.

"I like that . . . that's a good one. I'll have to remember that," Anthony complimented. "You wanta drive for awhile? We're gettin' close to the city and you know your way around these parts."

"Yeah, hom', pull off up here somewhere—I need to stretch a minute anyway."

The damp coolness of the night air was refreshing on my face. I took a big deep breath of the country-flavored molecules, and felt my blood start to circulate again. After a few jumping jacks and knee bends, we jockeyed back into position and headed north.

"Well, the lightnin's all behind us now . . . that oughta be good for the game tomorrow," I said as I adjusted the mirrors for my height.

"Yeah, I'm sure the players are glad. It ain't no fun in the mud, as you know," Anthony grimaced playfully.

"Nope," I agreed, "it makes every one of them yards seem like ten."

We settled into a comfortable quiet, each of us lost in our own thoughts. The humming of the tires and the engine sounds filled the interior with a soothing, syncopated rhythm. I could practically feel the wheels turning in Anthony's head. Searching . . . the poor kid was searching so hard. All I could do was tell him what it had been like for me. He still had to make his own way.

After a few miles, I felt myself getting sleepy. Even if he didn't want to talk anymore, I needed to, just to stay awake.

"You know, I've got another motto hangin' on my wall. Lloyd Jones says, 'The men who try to do something and fail are infinitely better than those who try to do nothing and succeed.' Every time I start to doubt myself, I think about that. Even after I played in the Super Bowl, I wouldn't wear my ring for about four years . . . it just laid in the drawer. Then one day, I let up on myself and realized that although I didn't do as much as I wanted to in that one game, my team had won the number of games it took to get there. The scoreboard told the rest. So I put it on my finger and it's been there ever since. It reminds me that victory and defeat are the same."

"What do you mean, the same? How can they be the same?" Anthony asked.

"Well, you know that old sayin' about it's not whether you win or lose, it's how you play the game? That was true for me, too. Sometimes my team would lose, but I'd play an exceptional game and feel good about it. Sometimes we'd win, like the Super Bowl, but I didn't do so great . . . so it boils down to how you feel about yourself. I always tried to make the big plays count. Of course, the risk of lookin' like a fool was always there, but that was part of the excitement, too. You take away the risk, and life goes flat, know what I mean?"

"I'm beginnin' to," Anthony said hesitantly, "but every time I think I've got the answers, somethin' changes and I'm right back in the quicksand," he said in exasperation.

"Yep, that's the way it goes!" I confirmed. "Change has a way of pullin' us out of the muck and mire so we can go on to higher ground. You just have to anticipate change and be ready, 'cause it is gonna come, no matter who you are or what you're doin'. I love change, man! I embrace it everyday. It keeps me from gettin' bored. It's sorta like exercisin' your body—it's necessary if you want to stay flexible and alive," I assured him.

The lights of the sprawling city reflected a rosy glow in the night sky. The clouds seemed to be huddling close to the car as if they, too, were listening for ways to end their turmoil.

"You know, Anthony, everything we have comes from a source bigger than ourselves. Our talents, our ideas, our dreams—these are gifts to be used in the service of this source. I call my source "God"—you might call yours somethin' else, but I know when I do God's work, no matter where I am, my life works! I used to think God's work was for ministers, missionaries, and monks. Now I'm a little bit wiser. I know that each of us has a position to play on this great cosmic team in life's infinite Super Bowl. You're gonna find your perfect place—you're gonna make it. You're gonna do just fine, 'cause like I told Lloyd, you're like a junkyard dog, and I'm bettin' on you!"

———◆———

When I dropped Anthony at his house after we got back from Oklahoma, he shook my hand and thanked me for the trip. We both knew it was decision time for him. He was about to walk through his front door and hopefully, he'd come out on the other side of the chasm.

Three nights later, I was home cooking a pork chop when the phone rang. I knew it was him before I answered the phone.

"So what did you decide, Anthony?" I asked quietly without saying hello.

"How'd you know it was me?" he laughed. "Are you psychic or somethin'?"

"Or somethin'," I replied, and waited.

"I'm not goin' back, Eddie," he said softly. "I'm gonna go forward with my business and I'm gonna be the best in Houston. I already called Buffalo and told 'em no."

I could hear the mixture of pride, fear, and determination in his voice. For the first time in a long time, my own voice wouldn't work at all.

My eyes, brimming with tears, found my favorite writing on the wall and Dantzig's words swam in the frame: *We cannot change the rules of the game, we cannot ascertain whether the game is fair. We can only study the player at his game; not however, with the detached attitude of a bystander, for we are watching our own minds at play.*

EPILOGUE

Eddie Gerald Hinton resides in Houston, Texas, and continues to operate and franchise Fly Clean International, Inc.

Mr. Hinton was appointed to The University of Oklahoma's Centennial Commission, whose 100 members were chosen for bringing distinction to their own careers and to The University. The Commission will plan and execute a year-long program of events in celebration of O.U.'s Centennial in 1990. He is also president-elect of the O.U. Club of Houston for 1988.

He is a frequent speaker throughout the South and Midwest; and is founder of Exec-U-Team, a non-profit organization whose purpose is to assist athletes in transition from the sports arena to the business world.

Mr. Hinton is also a regular participant in Celebrity Rodeo events, benefiting numerous charitable organizations; and is past-President of The Lone Star Polo Club.

For further information, Mr. Hinton may be contacted at P.O. Box 1395, Stafford, Texas 77477.

ABOUT THE AUTHOR

Lynne Washburn acquired twenty years' experience as a corporate executive and strategic planner in the trenches and in the boardroom of a highly successful national retail business.

In 1983, she started her own company to produce and publish media material for the coming era of global cooperation. Her first project was a public television special entitled *The New American Revolution*, depicting major changes in the sectors of business, health, education, and global relationships from 1776 to the present.

In her first book, *Locker Room to Boardroom*, she combines the reality of intellect with the poignancy of "heart" to explore the long-term effect of sports on the lives of America's most important role models, the professional athlete. Wherever the athlete goes, our children will follow.

COLOPHON

Production Consultant	– Gulf Publishing Company Houston, Texas
Production Executive	– Clayton Umbach, President Texas Publishers' Association
Writing Consultant	– Dr. Elizabeth Harper Neeld Author of best selling *Writing;* and best-selling audio-cassette album, *Yes, You Can Write*
Editors	– David Nathan, Author of *Lionel Richie, An Illustrated* *Biography* Timothy W. Calk, Senior Editor, Gulf Publishing Company
Production Consultant	– Jerele Neeld, President Centerpoint Press
Production Manager	– Carol Book Estes
Administrative Manager	– Wanda White
Graphics Manager	– Evelyn Ellison
Cover Design	– Neal D. Roper
Printing and Binding	– Walsworth Press, Inc.

Candle Publishing Company wishes to thank the following readers for their invaluable assistance in the development of the manuscript:

Sue Book	Patricia Brison	Nadine Brotemarkle
Bob Chapman	Patsy Dozier	Sonny Elliott
Evelyn Ellison	Noel Ellison	Judy Elswick
Amy Estes	Carol Book Estes	Larry Gardner
Dr. James Gauer	Linda Gauthier	Ellen Harrison
Betsy Hill	Rebecca Hoffman	Robert Hutson
Jill Jones	Mary Ellen Kirkpatrick	Bob Long
John Mackey	Rita McKigney	Keith Overby
Leslie Price	Russ Setzekorn	Arman Simone
Dee Sterling	Barry Warner	Charles Washburn
Lori Washburn	Mary Washburn	Sonja Washburn
Terry Washburn	Bob Wegmann	Wanda White
Pat Young		

PHOTO & QUOTE ACKNOWLEDGMENTS

Photos

#8, #9, #10—Courtesy of Lawton High School, 1965 LORE Yearbook

#11—Courtesy *Lawton* (Okla.) *Constitution-Press*

#12—1969 *Sooner* yearbook photo, courtesy Student Publications, The University of Oklahoma

#13—*The Oklahoma Daily*

#14—Staff photo by Jim Argo, Oklahoma Pub. Co.

#17—Cartoon by Richard Bibler

#18—Norman Transcript Photo

#19—U.S. Army Photo—Fort Polk, Louisiana

#23, #24 & "football" cover—UPI/BETTMANN NEWSPHOTOS

#27, #28, #31, #32, & "cowboy hat" cover—*Houston Chronicle*

Quotes

Quote by McCafferty (page 81) reprinted by permission of *The Baltimore Evening Sun*.

Quote by Dick Young (page 89) © 1971 New York News, Inc., reprinted with permission.

Quotes by "Doc" Hull (page 119), courtesy of Don Hull, a firm believer in free enterprise.

Quote by Lloyd Jones (pages 172–173), from *2715 One Line Quotations for Speakers, Writers, and Raconteurs*, p. 77.

ORDER FORM

LOCKER ROOM TO BOARDROOM: Super Bowl Player Eddie Hinton's
Strategies for Tackling Life's Choices, Challenges, and Changes

Please send me ___ copies of LOCKER ROOM TO
BOARDROOM @ $17.95 (hardcover) $ _____

Please send me ___ copies of LOCKER ROOM TO
BOARDROOM @ $12.95 (softcover) $ _____

           SUBTOTAL $ _____

Sales Tax: Texas residents add 7% sales tax   + SALES TAX $ _____

Shipping: Add $2.00 for EACH book.   + SHIPPING $ _____

          ORDER TOTAL $ _____

SEND BOOK(S) TO:

NAME: _____

ADDRESS: _____

CITY: _____ STATE: _____ ZIP: _____

☐ Check enclosed for full amount. (Payable to Candle Publishing Co.)$ _____
☐ Charge my ☐ VISA ☐ Mastercard account:

Account Number: _____ Card Expires: _____

Name as it appears on card (please print): _____

SIGNATURE: _____

(Postage/handling and applicable Texas tax will be added.)
My day-time phone number (in case there are questions about my order):

Area Code _____ Number _____

MAIL ORDER FORM TO:
CANDLE PUBLISHING COMPANY
Order Department B-1
P. O. BOX 5009-136   Toll-Free Order #:   1-800-255-4942
SUGAR LAND, TEXAS 77487-5009 Ordering Hours: 9:00–4:00 c.s.t.

BULK INQUIRIES WELCOME
SATISFACTION GUARANTEED
THANK YOU FOR YOUR ORDER!

"ASSIST-AN-ATHLETE" ORDER FORM

LOCKER ROOM TO BOARDROOM: Super Bowl Player Eddie Hinton's Strategies for Tackling Life's Choices, Challenges, and Changes

YES, I WANT TO "ASSIST-AN-ATHLETE" BY SENDING A GIFT COPY OF **LOCKER ROOM TO BOARDROOM** TO THE FOLLOWING PEOPLE WHO WILL ALSO BENEFIT FROM EDDIE'S STORY:

SEND BOOK(S) TO:

NAME: _____

Address: _____

City: _____ State: _____ Zip: _____

NAME: _____

Address: _____

City: _____ State: _____ Zip: _____

_____ copies of LOCKER ROOM TO
           BOARDROOM @ $17.95 (hardcover) $ _____

_____ copies of LOCKER ROOM TO
           BOARDROOM @ $12.95 (softcover) $ _____

                              SUBTOTAL $ _____

Sales Tax: Texas residents add 7% sales tax   + SALES TAX $ _____

Shipping: Add $2.00 for EACH book.   + SHIPPING $ _____

                              ORDER TOTAL $ _____

☐ Check enclosed for full amount. (Please make payable to Candle
   Publishing Co.) .... $ _____
☐ Charge my ☐ VISA ☐ Mastercard account:

Account Number: _____ Card Expires: _____

Name on credit card (please print): _____

SIGNATURE: _____
(Postage/handling and applicable Texas tax will be added.)

Name: _____

Address: _____

City: _____ State: _____ Zip: _____

MAIL ORDER FORM TO:
CANDLE PUBLISHING COMPANY
Order Department B-2
P. O. BOX 5009-136   Toll-Free Order #:   1-800-255-4942
SUGAR LAND, TEXAS 77487-5009   Ordering Hours: 9:00–4:00 c.s.t.

SATISFACTION GUARANTEED
THANK YOU FOR YOUR ORDER!